DANIEL LIBESKIND
COUNTERSIGN

For Nina

ЕЛ

XA

OLYMPIA   MECHANICAL   GARDEN   RESTAURANT   HAUSMEISTER CARETAKER

BE

Architectural Monographs No 16

DANIEL LIBESKIND
COUNTERSIGN

A.D. ACADEMY EDITIONS

Architectural Monographs No 16
Editorial Offices
42 Leinster Gardens London W2 3AN

ISSN 0141-2191

Editorial and Design Team
Andreas Papadakis (Publisher)
Andrea Bettella (Senior Designer)
Vivian Constantinopoulos (House Editor)
Annamarie Uhr

Photography
Hélène Binet, Uwe Rau and Leo Torri

Subscriptions
Mira Joka

Publisher's note
This book is a work in progress towards a major Monograph on the work of Daniel Libeskind. The volume has been designed in collaboration with the architect, and the material used here is a sample from the more extensive work which will be covered in the monograph to be published soon.

Author's note
I would like to thank my publisher Andreas Papadakis for his support and commitment to publishing this work.

Cover: Aleph Wing, Berlin 'City Edge'; *P1:* Berlin 'City Edge'; *P2:* Writing Machine, Three Lessons in Architecture; *P3:* The Extension to the Berlin Museum with the Jewish Museum; *P4:* Berlin 'City Edge'; *P8:* Berlin 'City Edge'; *P11:* Memory Machine, Three Lessons in Architecture

First published in Great Britain in 1991 by
ACADEMY EDITIONS
An imprint of the Academy Group Ltd
42 Leinster Gardens London W2 3AN

ISBN 1 85490 094 3 (HB)
ISBN 1 85490 097 8 (PB)

Printed and bound in Singapore

CONTENTS

Architecture, the very word has lost its reputation: how is it to defend itself? Both 'good and bad' days are now gone. The everyday architect is dead. His body useless unless it becomes manure or kindling for the fire which, after all, is based on what is 'no better'.

What is not alone is whole, both willing and unwilling to be named object. Once numbered and multiplied, this whole grew at the expense of zeroes into which it has stepped. One knows construction by destruction and codes ever since Eiffel changed leisure into fatigue. The road of Architecture does not have two directions but only one – meaning that eyes are better transformers than gears, when our understanding grates on matters which will be ever resistant, incomplete. Incompleteness being the trial of psyche; bridge over skill and intelligence.

Brightness of Form was a virtue when sleepy gods were doing the world's business and helping to prolong the season of All. But eventually their sons changed the rhythm of moving evening tides through errors – agents of justice – into nuclei visible on a dial. One of these is the daynight wintersummer warpeace. The other is too little to pinpoint since it is disguised as a city and known in each separate flavour of affliction.

The wisdom seen through the little hole cut in Knowledge appears as having been plotted in the course of history by all things other than modesty. Yet modesty alone constitutes the will named as *Father who is not I*, *That which is not world* or *All-not-in-one*.

What then is Architecture? Don't notice it. However, by supposing that force relates to looks, ie to the musical instruments still harbouring weapons, one can unhinge design of things and cities, releasing the 'more harmonious than seen' into each architectonic device whose life lies in killing. Deadly thinking: day in night time.

The same can be said of living the death of architecture which fake lips have reduced to 'youthful age'. What calls into being follows the thunder – process capable of reversal. Once joined by two lines and a semi-circle, Architecture becomes reducible to parts of speech or organs of the body. Hence 'co-operation' thoroughly overdetermines the position of the field and makes harmony into a separate or fourth element. As with knowledge the opening crisis is an anguished if inarticulate experience: partly lunar curse, partly the curled wool before its thread has been straightened.

The Vitruvian realm which limits Architecture to the Art of Building, the Construction of Machines and the Making of Time-pieces acts as the venerable liver which has been split into three and not the famous rail of Roussel on which I suspend the beginning of a circle or its violently cut end – half spurned, half poisoned. Then the doctor forgets to submit the bill to you and hands it to God, the Beautiful or the Good. (It should be a human being who sees things divine, ugly, good; better yet, a boy who will never be a 'man', as 'man' was never 'god'!)

If every construction were just smoke one's perception would not be restricted. But dates themselves are senses giving and receiving each other's small insanities. How to withstand the heart's desire – since editing gets what it wants – at the soul's expense?

Stirred like a delicious drink, the recess springs forward like hot wine mixed and seasoned by a boasting harlequin who created chess pieces and a separate playing board which consists in the one step upon which the foot does not slip even when frozen.

Life is to Architecture as Earth is to a watery physical force. The architect has been locked in a trunk while Architecture is staggering mindlessly to lift the load back home. By now, or soon, the sweat will evaporate and be forever lost (cubes have always been pre-historic). Thus emerges the wonderful order of a world no longer seen as the random gathering of things significant only when clumsy. A world in which each hair-pin, arcade or tribe can no longer posture in the mother's *sensus communis*. The shapes are cold, handwritten, dry: one simply cannot find their boundary in the East or in the profound fairy detector with an always extended arm.

It shall remain Unaccountable, faintly whispering – clear of illogic and logic, sure to reason on the course of heavenly bodies, the factor π, law-abiding men trying to derive absence from songs. What penetrates fools satisfaction. Humanity reposes while mighty defenders fight madness in words, gloomy origins of the igloo, the rough millennium whose thousand-year-old ray looks like a statue of a hero gossiping behind the fallen house.

Understanding is absent-minded. The unseen Design: an inorganic sediment. The Ephasians might as well rest, letting their city be governed by children.

Without ending (since the above is neither theory nor object), I believe that even the ugliest architecture is going to be clearer than the handsomest name or the wisest visage. Because what is less wide is more beautiful. To put it simply: god at a distance looks like a construction or an edifice, but only to those who have acquired form. The calculable always equals two times god.

ENERGIA IAENER G. *I Aener*

Giaener. Giaen erg **IAENE RGIAENE,** *rgiaene* **RGIAEN.** *erg Iaene.* Rgi, aen erg, Iaener! gia ener giaener. *Gia.* Ener G iae nergia, energia en erg iae, Nergi aen ergiaene? Rgi aen erg iaen Er giaen erg iaener giae Nergiae Ne rgiaene rgi aenergi ae nergi; Ae N, erg iaenergi ae nerg iaener, Gia energ iaenergiae ne rgi aener, Gia energ iaen'e gi aene rg iaen, Er giae ner giaen er gia ene? Rgi, aener gi aener, gia ene rgia ener Giae nerg iae ner g iae, Nergiaen erg iaenerg, iae, ne rgiaen er, Giaen erg iae ner giae, ner gia ene. Rgi aene rgiaen erg; iae ner giae, Ner gi aen erg ia Energia Ener gi a' ene rgiaene; rgiaene rg Iaen ergi ae nerg iae nergiae. Nerg iaenerg iae nerg iaener giaener, Giae nergia ene rgiaenergi aenerg. I ae ner gia ene; rgia energ l'ae rgiae Nerg i aenerg iae n ergia ene; Rgiae nergiaen ergi ae nergiae ner giae. Nerg iae nergia en erg iaen Ergia energ i aenergia ener giaenerg; l'ae nergi ae ner gi aene rg iaener; Gia ener giaene'r gi aener giaenerg Iaene rgiae nerg iaenergiae nergiae Ne rg iae nergiaen er giaen ergiaener Giaen ergi aen er gi aen ergiaener. Gi aener giaen ergi, aener giaen, erg iaen *Ene. Rgia ener gia* en? Eer'g iae nergia ener giae; Ne rgia en ergiae nergia en er giaene Rgiae ner giaen erg iaen ergi. A'en er Giaener. *Gia.* En Ergiaen, E;rgi aenergiae nergiae Nergi aene rg iaene. Rgiae ne rgi, Aener'g iaenerg ia ene'r giaene; rgi aene rg iaene, Rgi aenerg iaener. *Gia.* Ener giaenergi aener giae'n ergi Aene rgi aen ergiaen, erg iae nergia ene Rg ia energ iae ner. Giaenergi, ae nergi; Aen erg ia ene rg iaener gi aener-giaene, Rgi aener giae . Nergi'a energia en ergi aener Giaen ergiae rgiaen, ergi aener'g ia energ iaen.[*Ergzae* **NERGI AE.** *Nergiae Nergiae'n ergiae Nergi* **AENE** *rgi ae* **NER GIA** . *Ene R.* Giaenergia ene rgi A ene rgiaener giae; Nergia ene rgiaen er giaen ergi A ener giae Nergi aenergia ene rgiae nergia; ene rgia ener giaen Ergi aenergi aenerg iaenergi. *Aene.*Rg, iaen ergiae, Nerg iaene, rgi aenergi, ae nergiaen ergi aen'e rgi, Aenergia ene rgiaen ergia. En erg iaene, 'rgi aen, Erg iae nerg iaene rgiaenerg iae nergiaener giae. Ne'r giae'n ergiaenergia, en erg iae'n ergia, Ener giaenerg iaen erg iaen er giaen ergiae, Nerg iaener giaen ergiae nerg ia? Erg iaen erg iaen ergi'a ener. Gi Aenergi aene, R giaene, rgiaener gi aen ergia en ergia, *Nerg.*'Iaene rg Iaenrg'i aene? *Rgia.* Energia en Ergiaener, Gia energi aenergiaene rg iae nergiaenergi, Aen ergiaene rg iaene rgiae. *Nerg.* Iaen erg ia Energ ? *Iaen.* Er, giaene, R'gi ae Nenrg. *Iaen.* Ergi, A ener giaener.

MICROMEGAS, 1979

'. . . it was the *reflection* of the inquisitor's eyes which still remained in his own, and which he had refracted in two spots on the wall.'
Villiers de L' Isle Adam, *Torture Through Hope*

Architectural drawings have in modern times assumed the identity of signs; they have become the fixed and silent accomplices in the overwhelming endeavour of building and construction. In this way, their own open and unknowable horizon has been reduced to a level which proclaims the *a priori* coherence of technique. In considering them as mere technical adjuncts, collaborating in the execution of a series made up of self-evident steps, they have appeared as either self-effacing materials or as pure formulations cut off from every external reference.

While the classical axiomatic of architectural drawing elaborated its usefulness within an overall theory of order, by beginning with well-established theories of representation and attempting to unify them, contemporary formal systems present themselves as riddles – unknown instruments for which usage is yet to be found. Today, we seldom start with particular conditions which we raise to a general view; rather we descend from a general system to a particular problem. However, what is significant in this tendency (where the relation between the abstract and the concrete is reversed) is the claim which disengages the nature of drawing, as though the 'reduction' of drawing were an amplification of the mechanisms of knowledge; an instrument capable of revealing, at a stroke, new areas of the 'real'.

There is an historical tradition in architecture whereby drawings (as well as other forms of communication) signify more than can be embodied in stabilised frameworks of objectifiable data. If we can go beyond the material carrier (sign) into the internal reality of a drawing, the reduction of representation to a formal system – seeming at first void and useless – begins to appear as an extension of reality which is quite natural. The system ceases to be perceived as a prop whose coherence is supported by empty symbols, and reveals a structure whose manifestation is only mediated by symbolism.

An architectural drawing is as much a prospective unfolding of future possibilities as it is a recovery of a particular history to whose intentions it testifies and whose limits it always challenges. In any case, a drawing is more than the shadow of an object, more than a pile of lines, more than a resignation to the inertia of convention.

The act of creation in the order of procedures of imagination, here as elsewhere, coincides with creation in the objective realm. Drawing is not mere invention; its efficacy is not drawn from its own unlimited resources of liberty. It is a state of experience in which the 'other' is revealed through mechanisms which provoke and support objective accomplishments as well as supporting the one who draws upon them. Being neither pure registration nor pure creation, these drawings come to resemble an explication or a reading of a pre-given text – a text both generous and inexhaustible.

I am interested in the profound relation which exists between the intuition of geometric structure as it manifests itself in a pre-objective sphere of experience and the possibility of formalisation which tries to overtake it in the objective realm. In fact, these seemingly exclusive attitudes polarise the movement of imagination and give an impression of discontinuity, when in reality they are but different and reciprocal moments – alternative viewpoints – of the same fundamental, ontological necessity.

We cannot simply oppose the formal to the non-formal without at the same time destroying the mobility, variation and effectiveness incarnated in the very nature of formalism. From a certain point of view everything is formalism; the distinction between 'perspective' and 'figure' (depth and flatness) – which seems definitive – branches off and distributes itself over layers of intentionality which in reality show a continuity more than a difference. In a parallel analogy, all seems to be supported by the empirical significance of signs themselves, which magnify appearances by reducing structure to them.

My work attempts to express this inadequacy at the heart of perception for which no (final) terms are provided; a lack of fulfilment which prevents manifestation being reducible to an object-datum. Only as horizons, in relation to time, can forms appear in this exploration of the 'marginal' where concepts and premonitions overlap. There is a presentation, but always according to the mode of imperfection; an internal play in which deferred completeness is united with a mobilised openness. The work remains an indefinite series because this dialectic cannot be halted. As such, these drawings and collages develop in an area of architectural thinking which is neither a physics nor a poetics of space.

Because the 'geometry of experience' is only a horizon of potential formalisation and we find it already inserted into that other horizon of desire and intuition, the task of essential clarification, as I see it, becomes the systematic and dynamic transmutation of movements; an exchange between abstract cyphers, exhausted in their own objectivity and hardened in fixed signs, and concrete contingencies responsive to the permanent solicitations of a spontaneous appeal.

An authentic abstraction gives us what is most unique in incomplete but formalised levels of grasping objects. It does so because at first uniqueness is given in an impure fashion, blended as it is with elements representing categories of experience which must be progressively extracted from the general alienation of over-qualified intuition of spatial structure. This 'purification' attempts, through a series of successive steps, to realise the elimination of intuitive content and numerical relations, and leads to ever more encompassing (spherical) possibilities of configuration.

But through an enigmatic reversal, one discovers in this ascent (or escape?), through the 'funnel' of an increasingly precise effort of projection, a regression towards the unique and primordial condition of metrics. The vectorial 'going beyond' is, at the same time, a deepening spiral movement which exposes this transgression as a moment of a concentric approach. In this sense, an overall envelopment neutralises tension and reveals a foundation both of continuity and change: a homogeneous state pervades even the most complex antinomies.

Most of all, however, I am a fascinated observer and a perplexed participant of that mysterious desire which seeks a radical elucidation of the original pre-comprehension of forms – an ambition which I think is implicit in all architecture. If there is true abstraction here (as opposed to generalisation) it is not achieved by the elimination of contents through a gradual deployment of an increasing emptiness, but is rather an isolation of structural essence, whose manifestation in two dimensions illuminates all the sub-systems of projection (for example, three-dimensional space).

Edmund Husserl's *The Origin of Geometry* has been an inspiration to me in all these 'researches'. Understanding that the historical genesis of geometry evolved from the problems of land-surveying (as calculus originated from the study of movement, or statistics from the study of collectivities), I have become increasingly aware of the fact that the disclosure of the first horizon (outlining the space of initial encounters) also guarantees the 'leakage' in the project of objectification. The same structures which we have already experienced in a confused and pre-reflective situation are continually transposed to a reflective realm where they open the way for ever more elaborated descriptions. It is not a matter of piling superimposed hierarchies one on top of another; rather, the trajectory of intentions transposes content into operation and at the same time displaces descriptive geometry by the structural. The transformation of object into operation imposes a temporal dimension on this process; a process whose meaning is not arbitrary and yet is not predetermined either.

The invisible ground from which it is possible to scaffold moving layers of construction enables one to recover modes of awareness quite removed from the initial hypothesis of rationality. These drawings seek to reflect, on a deeper level of consciousness, the inner life of geometrical order whose nucleus is the conflict between the Voluntary and the Involuntary. Once again this duality (like that of realism-formalism) appears as an unsurpassable condition pointing to a dynamic ground which testifies to an experience receiving only as much as it is capable of giving; draws only that which allows itself to be drawn into.

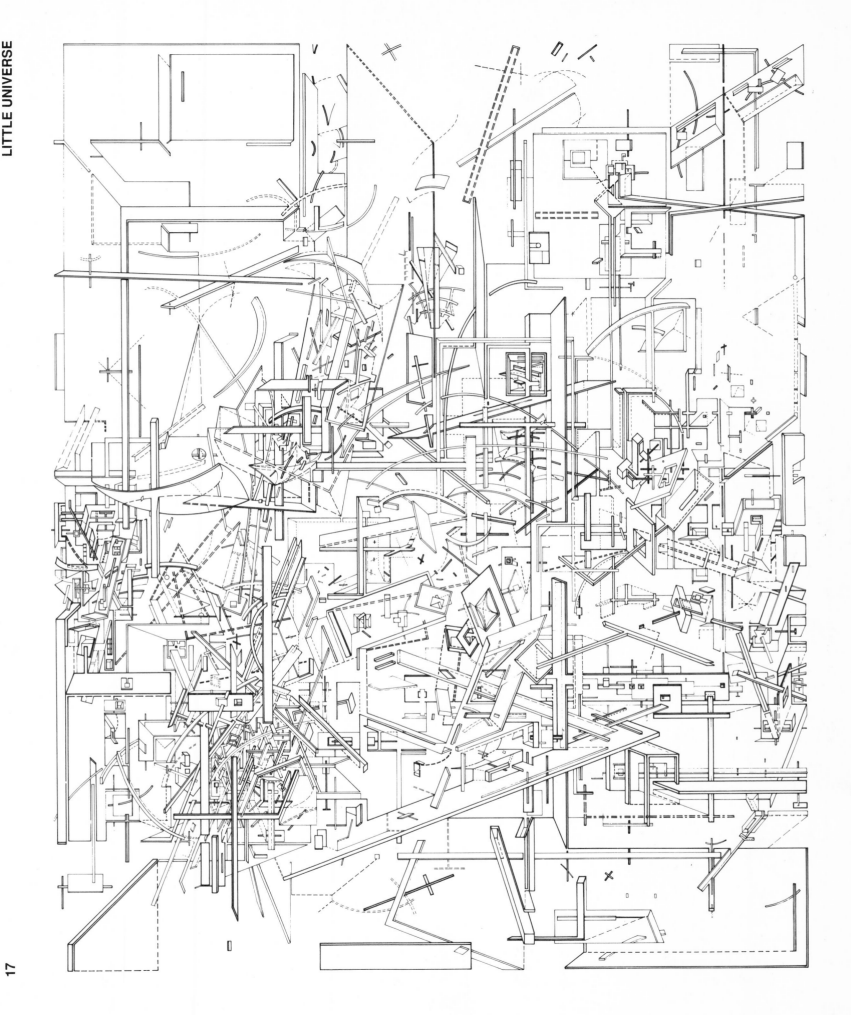

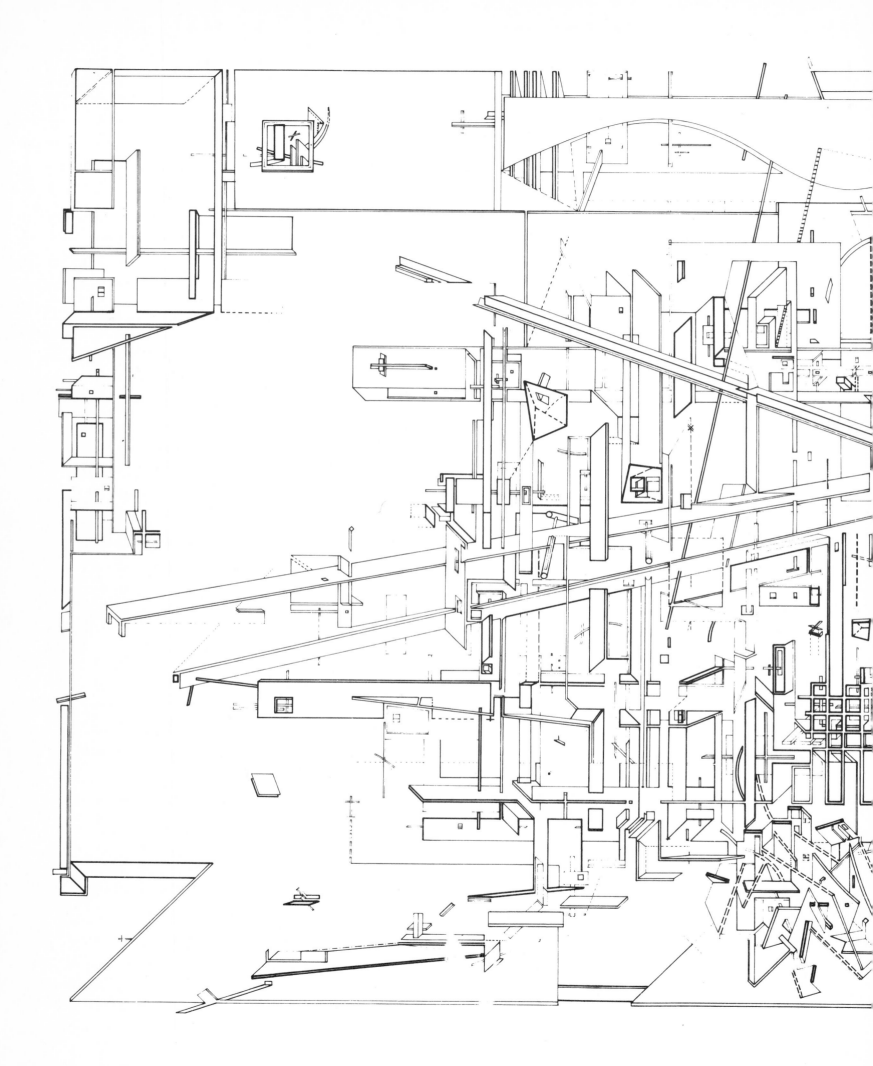

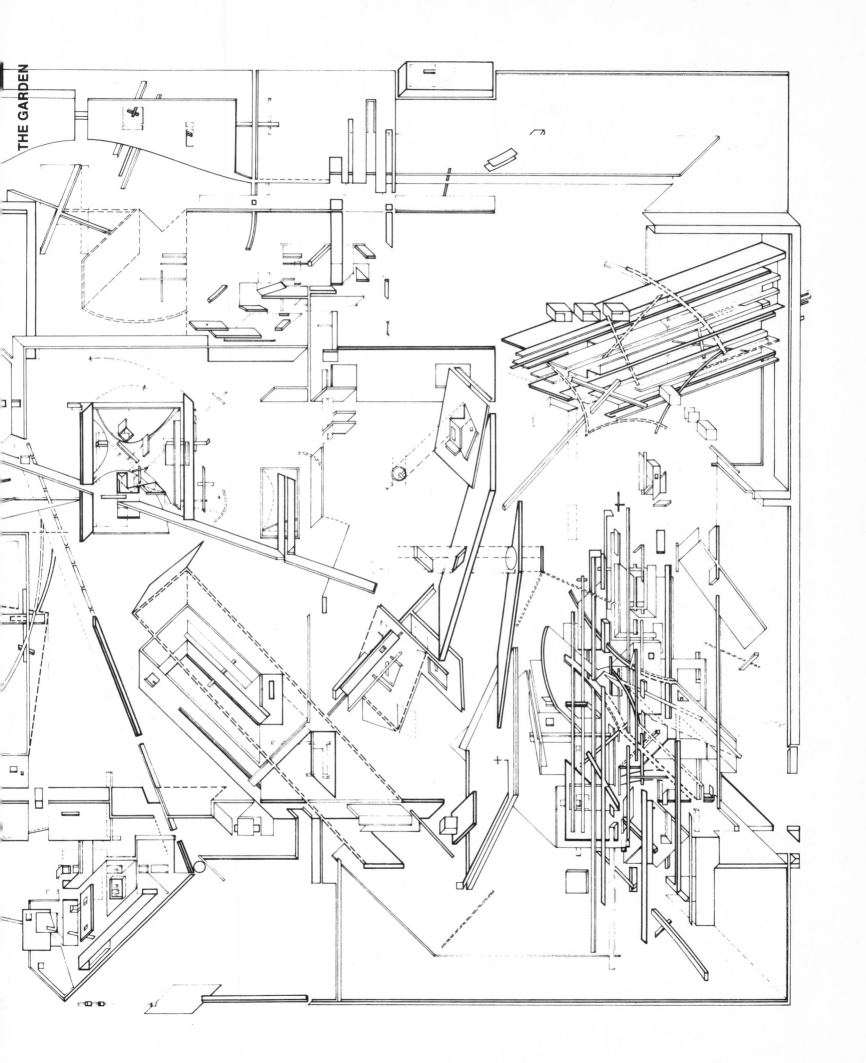

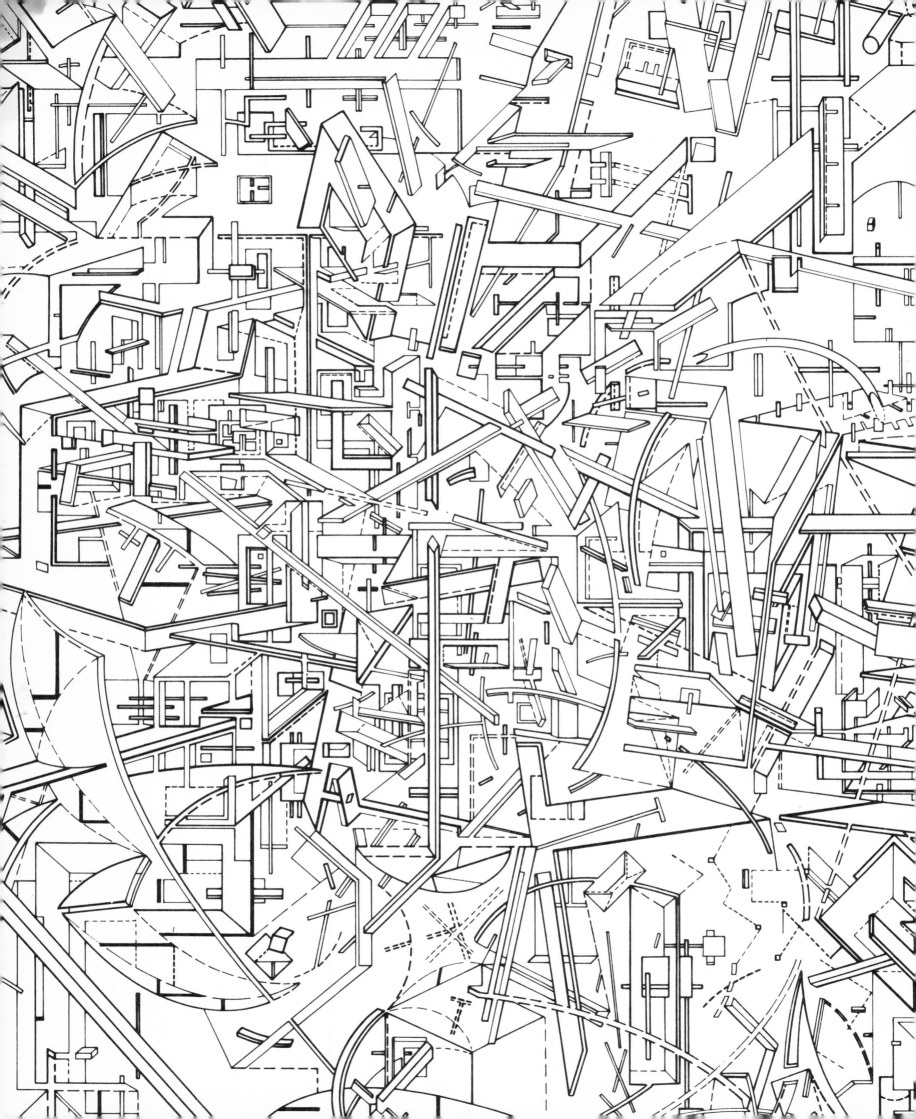

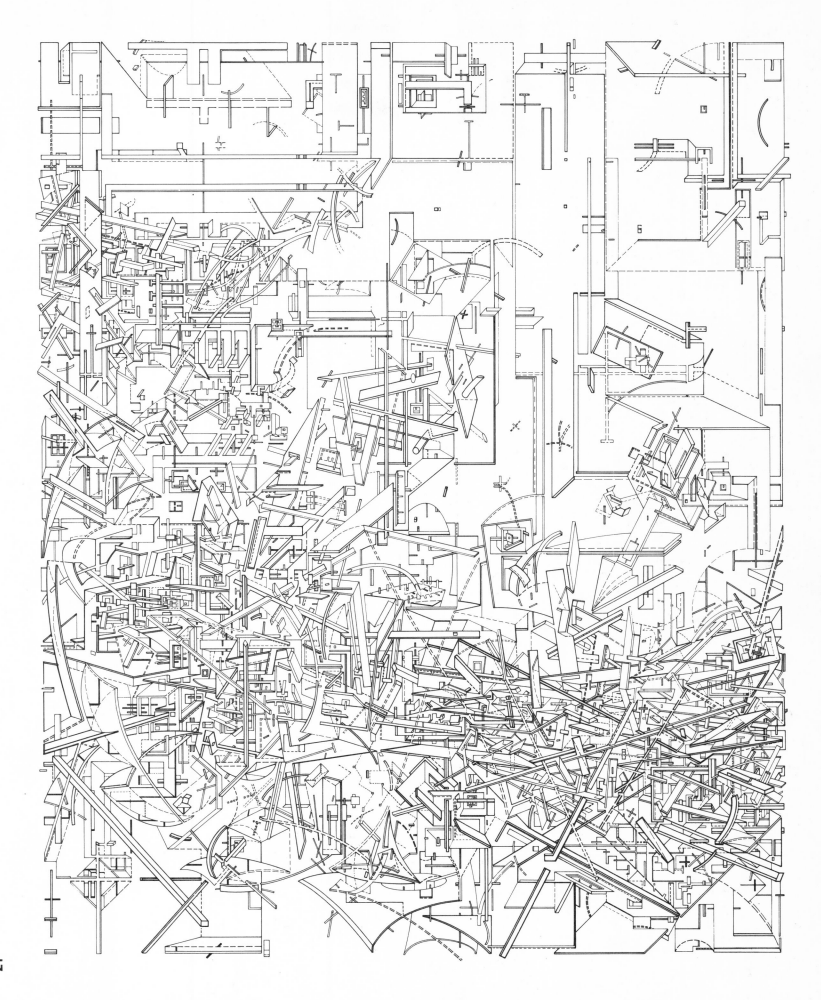

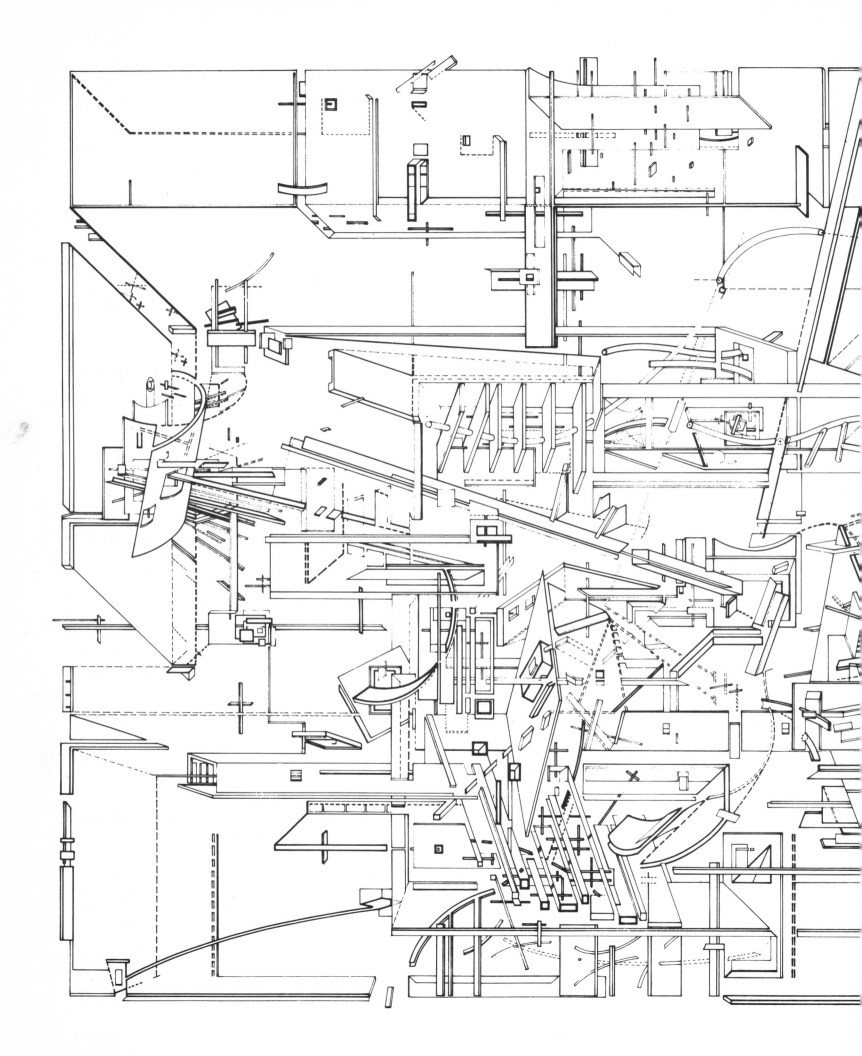

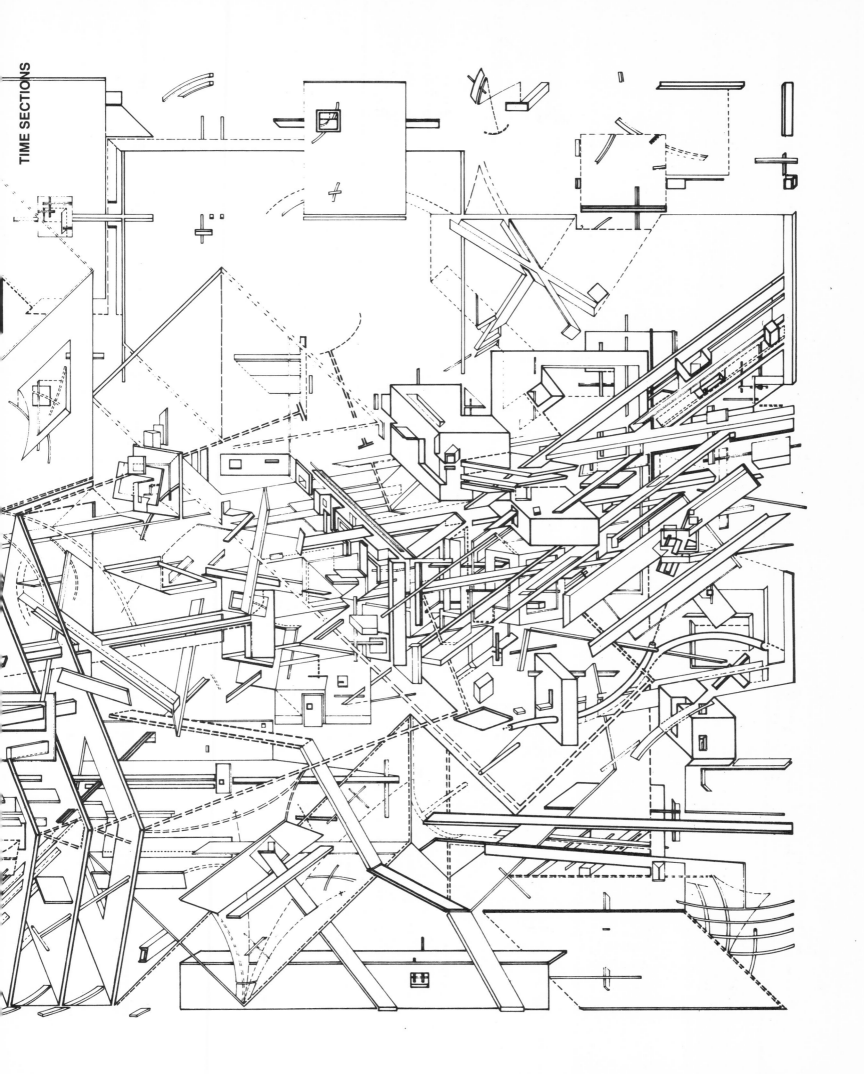

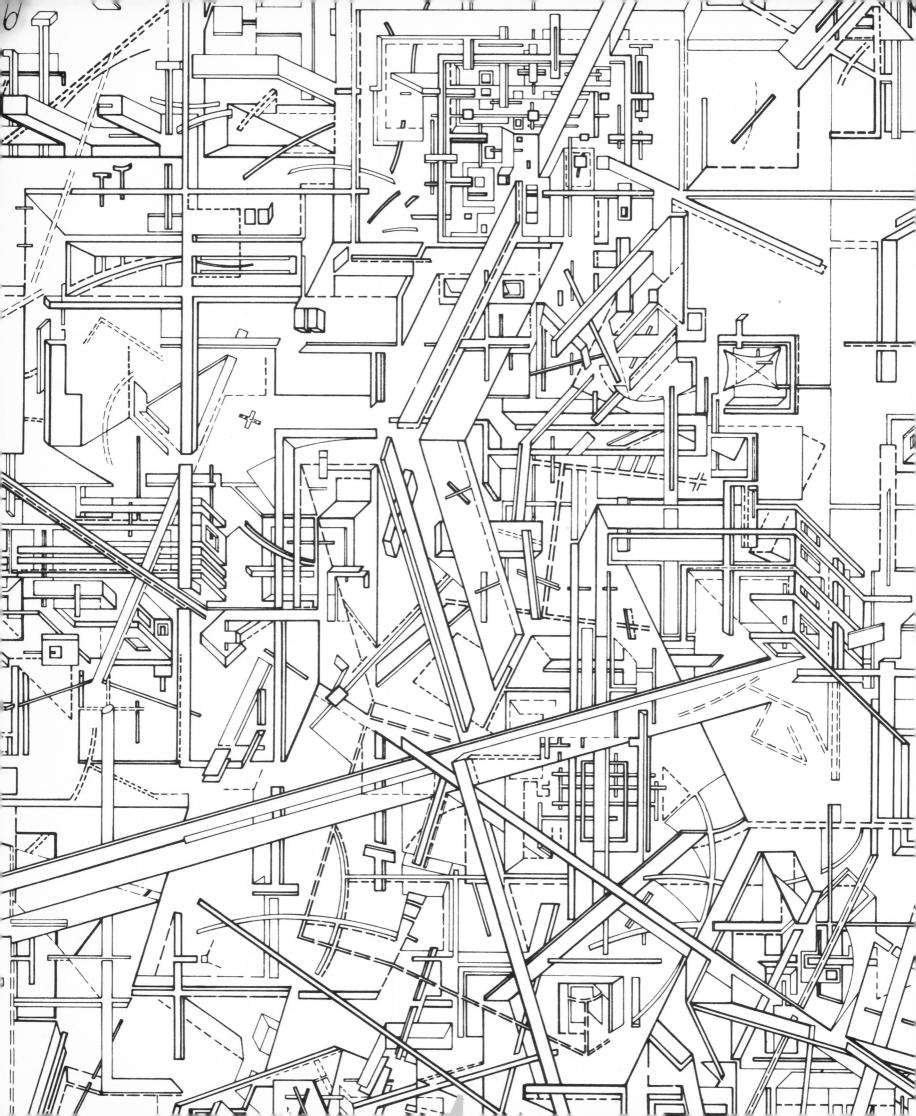

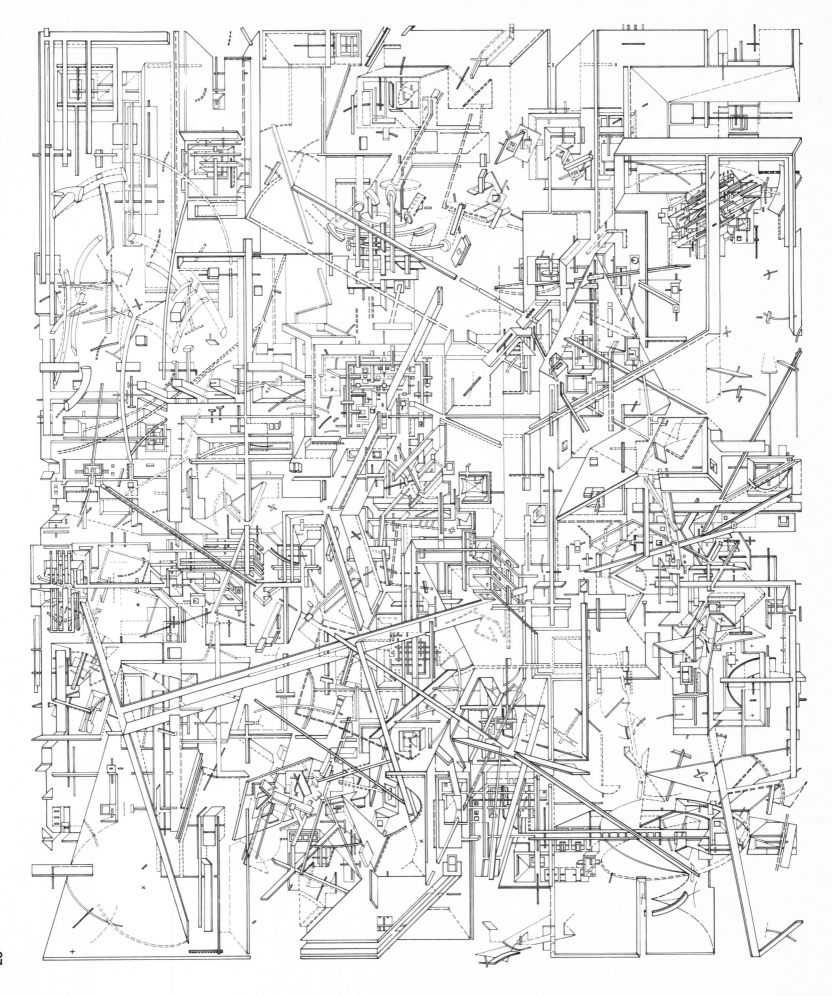

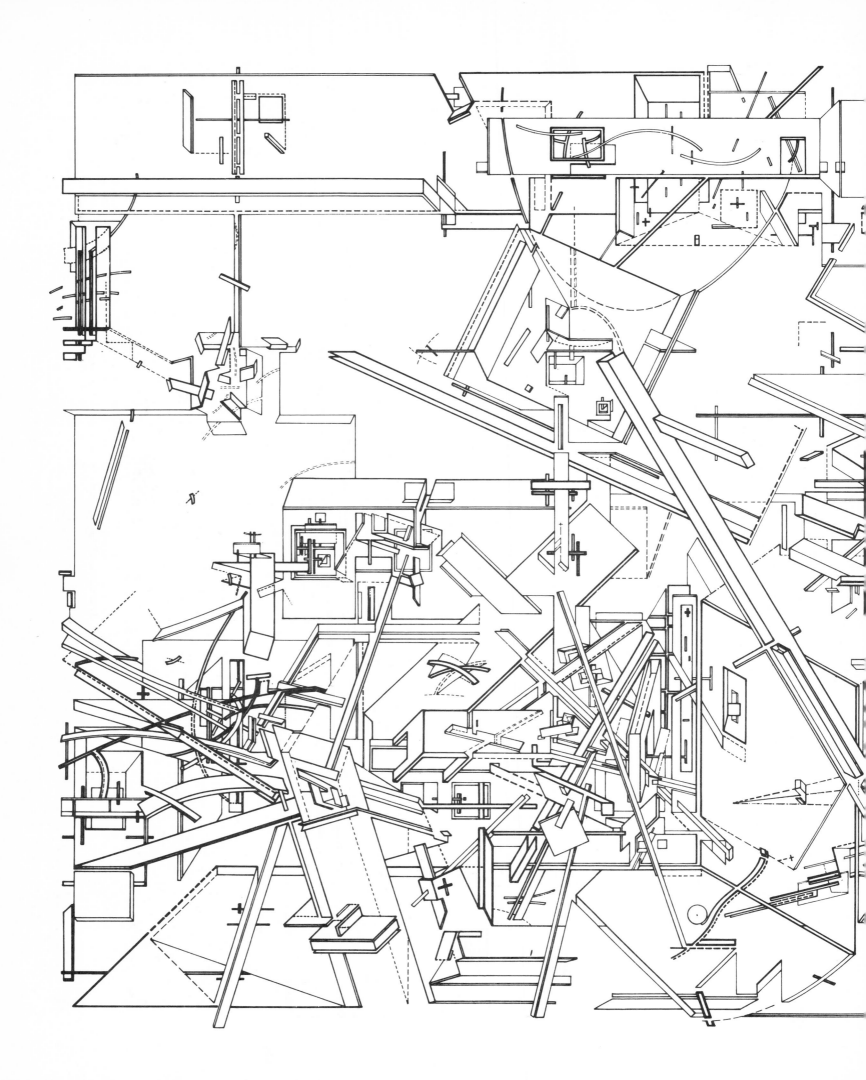

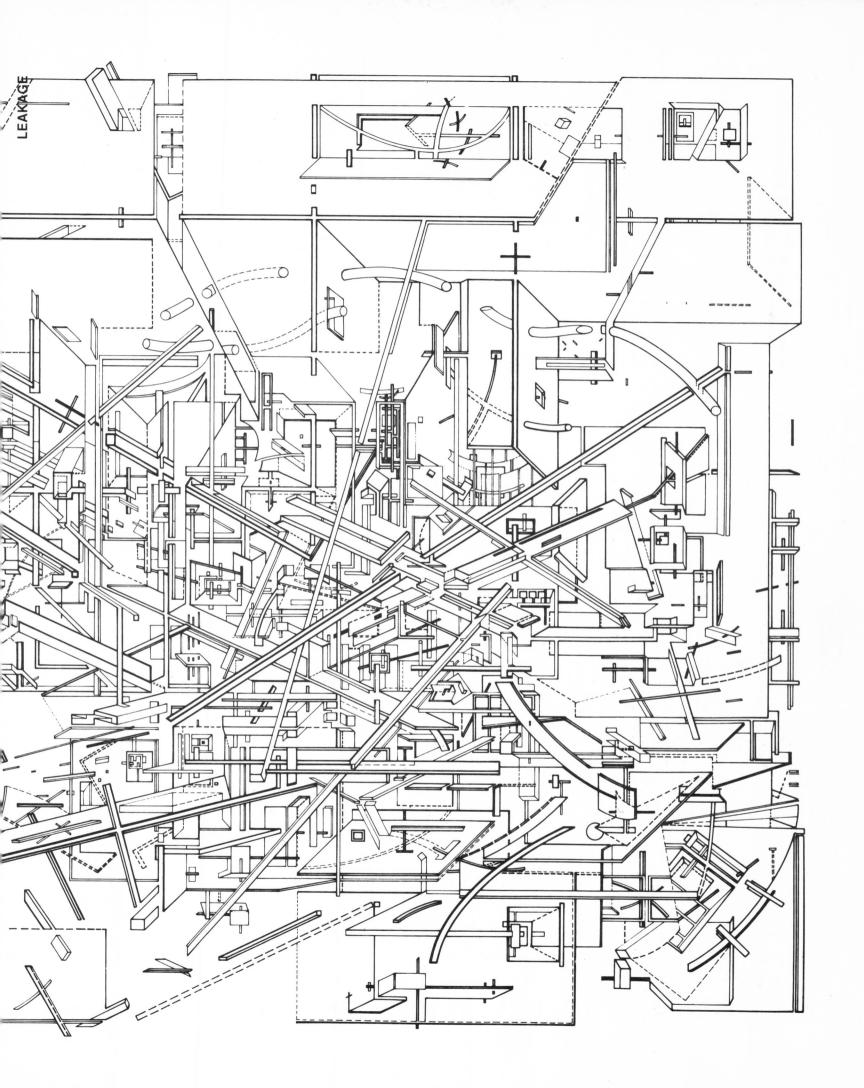

LEAKAGE

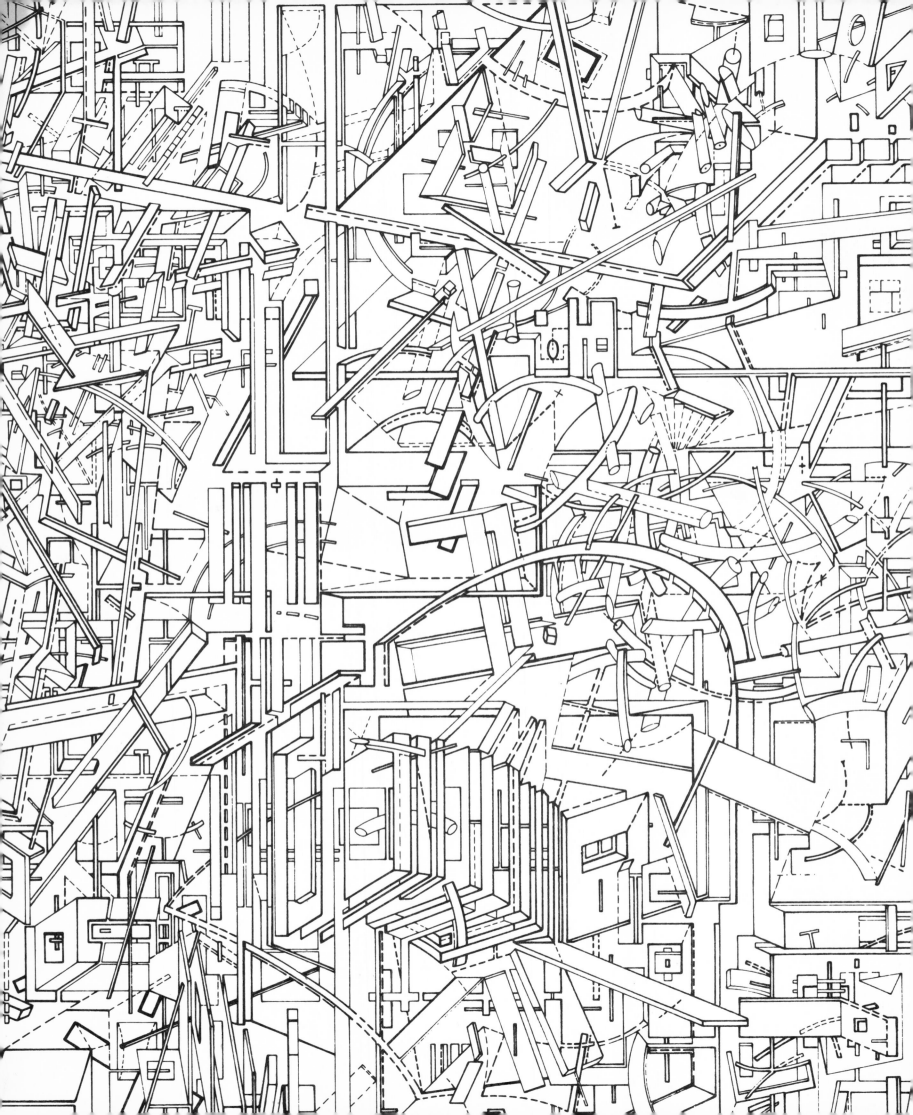

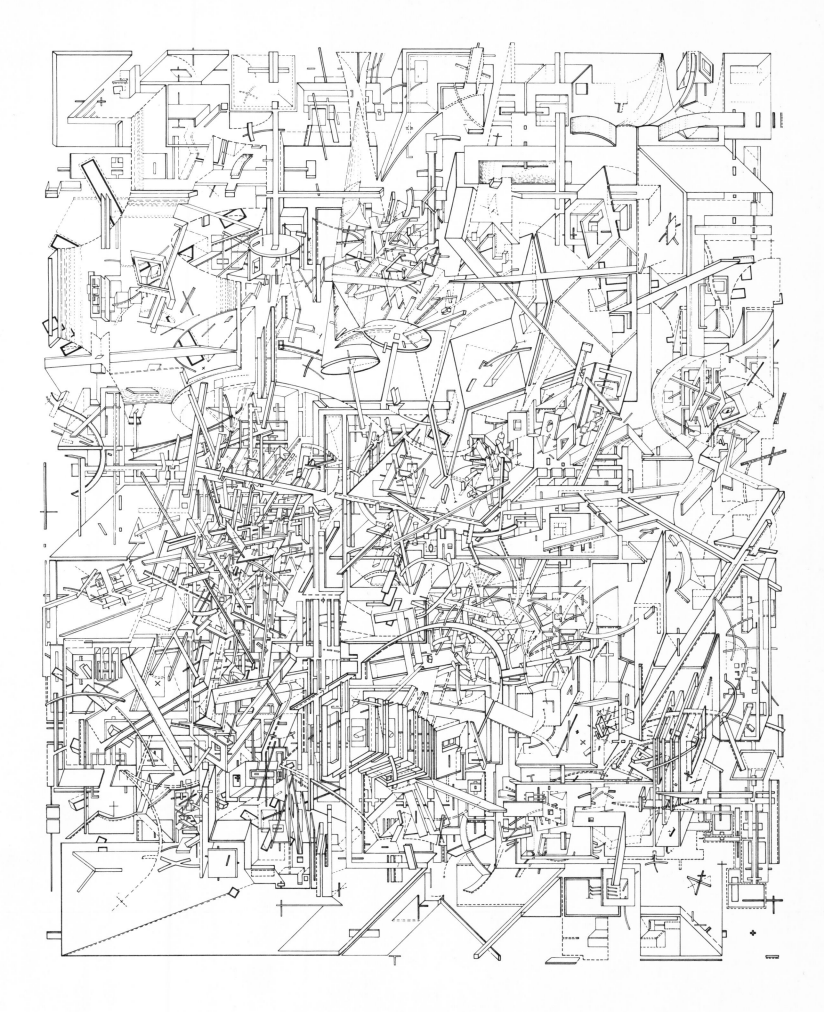

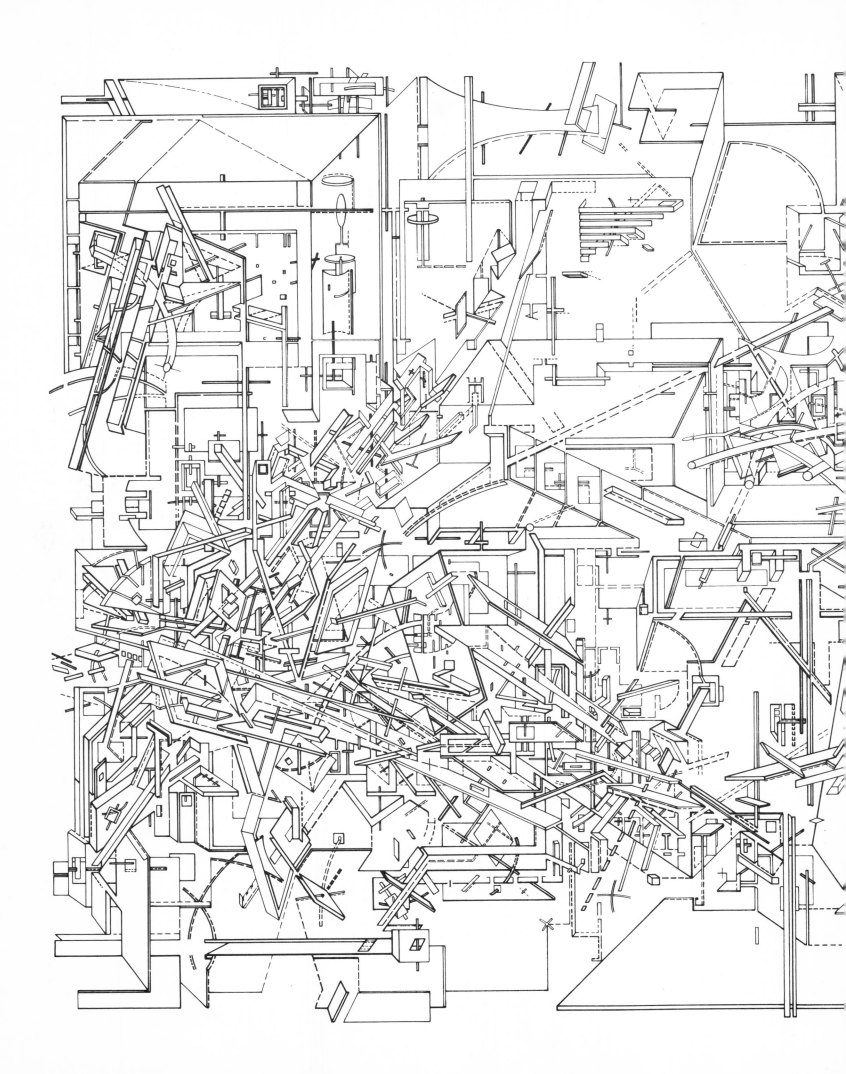

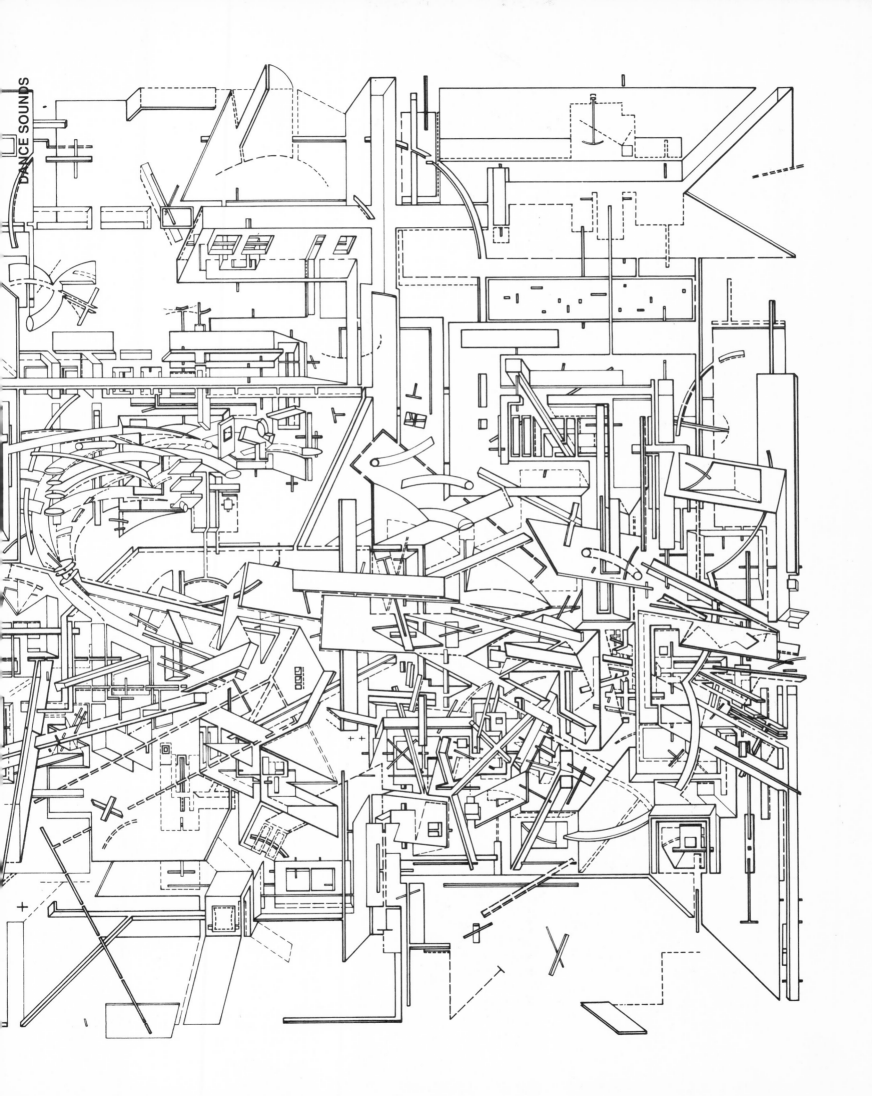

THIS IS:
OF A LIMITED
EDITION OF **30**
NUMBERED AND SIGNED
PORTFOLIOS

№:

micromegas
THE ARCHITECTURE OF END SPACE

D. LIBESKIND

"About the four hundred and fiftieth year of his age, or latter end of his childhood, he dissected a great number of small insects not more than one hundred feet in diameter, which are not perceivable by ordinary microscopes, of which he composed a very curious treatise, which involved him in some trouble."

VOLTAIRE

MICROMEGAS

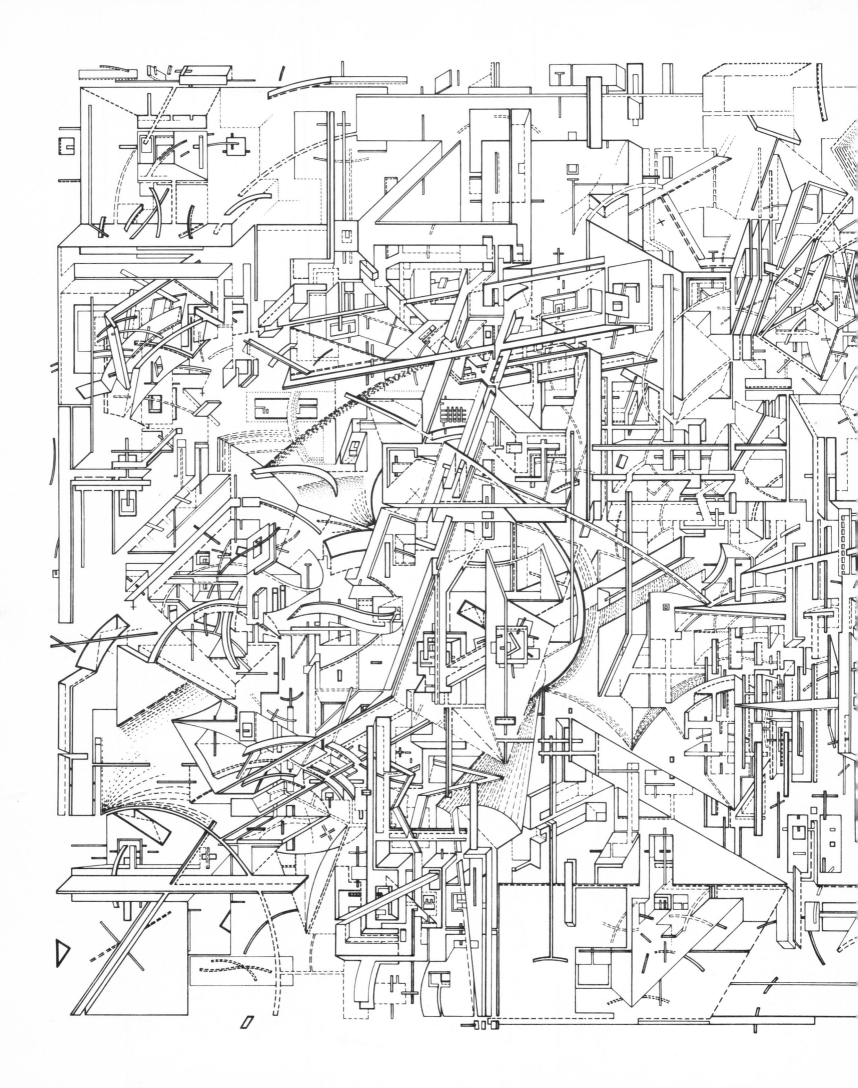

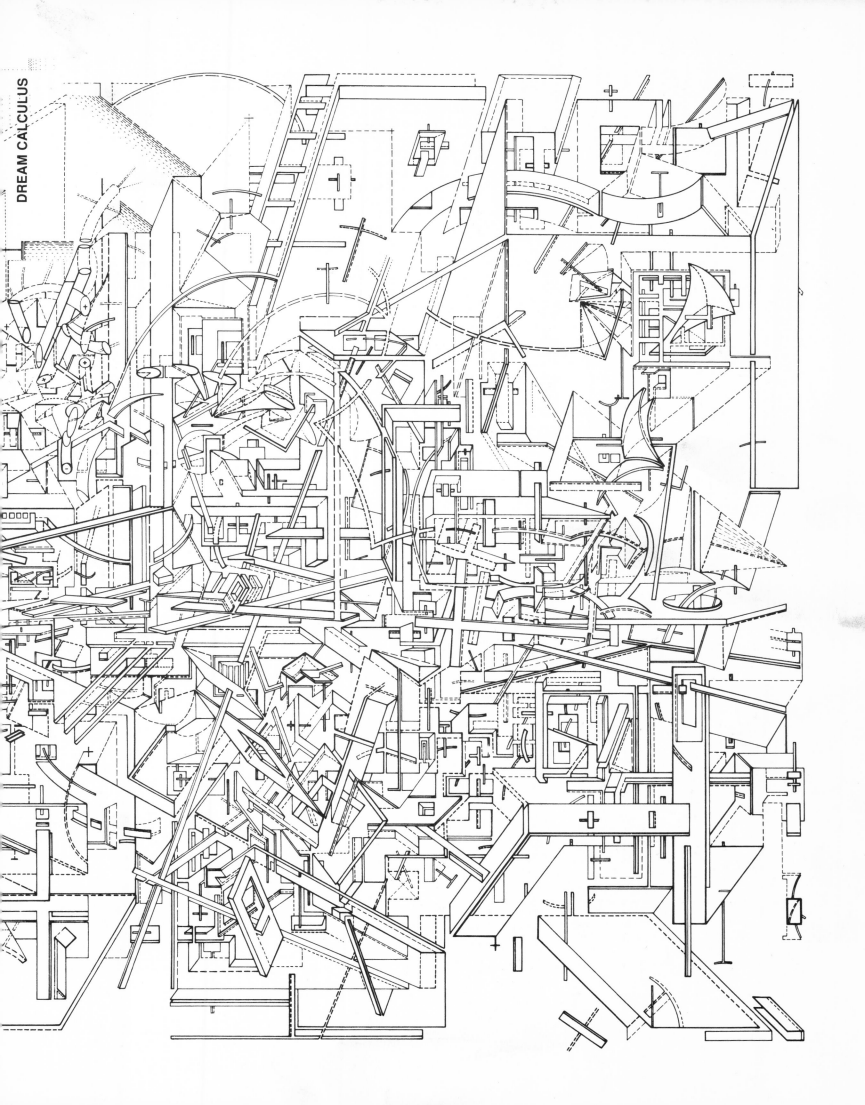

THREE LESSONS IN ARCHITECTURE, 1985

I believe that practising architecture today, teaching architecture today, being a student of architecture today, entail very different consequences than they did even a hundred years ago. I think all of us are at a different stage of possibility, of development of the modern world. I believe that architecture has entered its end. That is not to say that architecture is finished, but that architecture has entered an *end condition*. I think that all those who practise architecture, whether knowingly or unknowingly, feel in some way that something has come to an end, but what it is, is very difficult to say since it is not in the realm of *objects*. Therefore, I will try to speak as clearly as I can of something about which it is not easy to speak, because it is not one more thing which can be found in the catalogue of the world.

In any case, what I will try to speak about is a kind of *difference* – to use Derrida's word – and I will try to make this difference apparent by saying only one thing: that if equilibrium could have been attained, it would have been attained a long time ago. Equilibrium could have been attained under two conditions only. One is that reality would have been indeterminate or indistinct, a kind of Heisenberg/Mondrian postulation that equilibrium is achievable within a context of indeterminacy. This did not happen. On the other hand, equilibrium could have been achieved by postulating a global meaning of the world, a boundless but finite meaning, which is to say the meaning of Einstein, the meaning of mythology, the meaning of the centred world. But, needless to say, neither of these realities have been experienced, and they won't be. So what there is is the shape of space of the world which on a permanent basis produces a destabilised, let's say an eternal, movement of imperfection and difference. It is this shape of space about which I would like to speak and explore in a very tentative manner because no language exists for it today. No language has been agreed upon in which to discuss such a phenomenon. I would like to draw a diagram for you to refer to, because it's a kind of schema of my small discourse here.

What I would like to illustrate with this diagram, synoptically and synthetically, is a schema of a project I made with some friends some time ago entitled 'Three Lessons in Architecture', and presented in an Italian urban setting. It's a project that I did for a problem in Venice. I did not choose to address this problem by simply providing another craft, ideological or industrial solution. I chose instead to present an alternative solution by exploring participatory reality and to present those who ask the question with a participatory experience in which the problem of architecture might come into focus on the one hand, and some part of it might fall into oblivion on the other. I chose to address the urban problem of Palmanova (a city which exists in northern Italy in the Veneto region).

I presented the organisers of this programme with a piece of equipment, really one big movement in three parts. I will show it to you in three moments of the machine – the moment of reading, the moment of remembering and the moment of writing architecture. And I will start at some point, and end at some other point, but please remember that I'm really addressing this diagram as a totality. One could in fact start anywhere and one could end anywhere. It's a big circle of interpretation, not necessarily a vicious circle, but a circle that, by going through its own presuppositions, in some sense destroys and obliterates the problem of the given as it also exposes other dimensions of architecture. The three lessons that I have offered here are the three lessons of architecture: A) reading architecture, and its equivalent, the reading machine; B) the lesson in the present remembering architecture, and the memory machine; C) writing architecture, and its equivalent, the writing machine. So these are pieces of metaphysical equipment (as they don't really do anything, they are in another realm) which propose a very curious path, because as I said earlier, architecture was, from its very beginning, at its end. At the end it's possible to retrieve in some sense the whole past and future destiny, because the end, of course, is nothing in the future, nor is it anything in the past, nor is it anything in the present – it is simultaneously on all three levels. The three machines propose a fundamental recollection of the historical vicissitude, in particular of Western architecture. They constitute a single piece of equipment and are mutually interdependent. Each is a starting point for the other. The purpose of this equipment is to release the end to itself; not to take the end, but to release the end to itself.

I think the objects in architecture are only residues of something which is truly important: the participatory experience (the emblem of reality which goes into their making). You could say that everything we have is that kind of residue. It is this experience that I would like to retrieve, not the object.

By the way, making machines, I discovered as I was doing this project, is an old task. Everybody needs machines. Vitruvius says that first of all an architect should make a machine – it is more important than making a city. Then he says you should also make a theatre and other things. Alberti says this as well. When I read Vitruvius and Alberti and they said every good architect must first make a machine to do architecture, I thought that if I'm going to be a good architect I must follow the tradition to its end. So I tried to do it in a particular way. We wanted to retrieve reading architecture, so we made this first machine. I have to say what is involved in reading to try to become a pure believer even in architecture. I know it's an experimental state. It's an experimental being I'm describing, not an experimental object. To try to become the pure medieval craftsman – that's really the object of this exercise. To make something in a way which is made only on one's knees; which is made through complete faith in the transcendence of architecture, of the text, of reading; which is made by a total faith in the craft; which rejects all modern techniques and technology; which rejects modern thinking about architecture. So we did it that way. We got up at the crack of dawn, four o'clock in the morning. We built this machine in a small place without any power tools, just with hand tools; with no electricity, just with candlelight. We went to bed early because with candlelight you can't work late. And we did it in silence because there is nothing to talk about when you work like that.

I feel it's the very notion of architecture. One always dreams, and I'm sure you have dreamt about it too, what it was like, and what it would be like to build this way. And of course, one must reconstruct this experience because how else does one make a circle without a ruler – with just a plumb line and compass? I tried to make simply one circle, and to do it in that way, full of faith, and to get the experience as close as possible to this loaded experience of the monastic faith in the craft of making. Therefore, lesson A teaches the almost forgotten process of building, which really has not yet come to complete fruition. I would say that the medieval process is still coming to an end today – it has not been finished. A certain technique was created, one which also brought a revolution of the word; a revolution of text. This archeological reconstruction (cities like Palmanova, military ideas in architecture and of engineering) and this will to power is disclosed by thinking about architecture and particularly by having no faith in its reality. I never knew about this weak point. Only when I started doing the project did I discover that the weapons of architecture and the weapons of the world did not originate in the Renaissance, they originated in the monastery. The machine gun, the parachute and the atomic bomb are not the inventions of Leonardo da Vinci, they are inventions of Thomas Aquinas and even earlier spirituality. I tried to become that architect who would be commissioned by a monastery and who would then deliver both the non-objective and the objective counterpart of the purified, holy experience. So I made a gear. And then I made many gears. Please remember they are made with a chisel. It's hard to polish things without sandpaper. I made these detours because I would like you to use these machines. Now, these machines were meant to be used since a machine is not something to look at; these are not aesthetic objects. I offered them to the citizens of Palmanova, the city for which I made the project. I suggested to the organisers of this competition that these three pieces of equipment be placed in the middle square of Palmanova, and that not just the architects but all the citizens who passed through this Piazza would use it. They could determine what the problem was and the possible solution to it.

I had never done any work like this before; it was all new for me. And the experience of it is like that – you have to pull or push the wheel; that's important. And because the wheel is heavy it creaks. If you were to sit at it you would push or pull it. This machine has many axles and many, many gears which are both hidden and revealed. It has shelves, and the whole mechanism is intended to support eight words. So there are eight words for which this mechanism is a support. Now, the words are very light because words are light; they don't weigh much. These eight words are especially light because I sought words which are no longer readable in the text of architecture – words which cannot be remembered or written down. I placed these eight, light words and made them into books to give them slightly more substance. I wrote eight books. I made the eight books by hand like the monks – made the paper, bound the books, and placed them into this big wheel. And what is interesting is that light as the books and the words are, they actually completely crush the weight of these axles made out of wood. In crushing the weight of the axles they expose two things: the reader and the movement of the wheel, which of course revolves and then comes back to its own starting point, like all wheels do.

There are ninety-two wedges and glueless joints, no energy of a contemporary kind. The machine seeks to represent the triumph of the spirit over matter, of candlelight over electrical light or darkness. It's made solely from wood as are the books. You will recognise that a wheel is always gigantic, no matter how small. This one is very big. It is a Vitruvian, Albertian humanistic wheel of fortune suitable for the diagonally crucified humanist of Raphael and Leonardo, for whom I really built it. The square intersecting with the circle. I would have liked to make it for Thomas Aquinas; perhaps he would have bought this piece for himself. It's a device good for comparative reading of the architectural text. Rather than shuttling to your desk and looking for authoritative things as those monks always did who were looking for the right book to verify the eighth book or the first book, I placed the books in the wheel so that comparisons could easily be made. And in being easily made they could also reveal the tautological nature of the architectural text at its end. The text of architecture is a tautological text, which means that it says the same thing at the end as it said at the beginning, because the beginning was its end already. In short, a chamber of revolutions. The word revolution is used here in its etymological sense: a revolutionary machine because it revolves, and with each revolution comes about the revolution of the text which is propelled by it.

It's difficult to show a book in a picture because a book is meant to be read. This is the first book I wrote, and strangely funny because it was stolen. Five minutes after it was presented for perusal of the public, the book was stolen, and the organisers of the Venice Biennale came to me and said: 'Look, the book was stolen, but since it's a printed book, you have another copy of it.' And I said: 'No, I won't!' because if you are really a monk you don't mass produce anything. You use the technology to do one thing only; so you print. You use the whole resourcefulness of that monastic faith to do a singular act only, and always the only one – the same singular act over and over again. So I don't have this book anymore. The book on ideas is missing, but there are still other books remaining and they are all different. They have different thicknesses. Some of the books are five hundred pages long. The pages are handmade and can be read. Someone asked me: 'Do you read these books?' Yes, and I have seen other people read them. So there are eight books. Somebody else asked me: 'Why eight books?' I discovered why while re-reading *Don Quixote*. You've read about the great knight, Don Quixote in his paper visor, going to fight against the injustice of the whole world. Cervantes says that Don Quixote met only one gentleman in his travels in Spain. In all his time (because he was old by the time he died) he met only *one* gentleman. He said it was the gentleman in green; he was a gentleman because he travelled, and he travelled with a satchel of only eight books. Clearly Cervantes already had more than eight books in the sixteenth century, and I certainly have more than eight books in my library. I made this project in order to get rid of my books, because I decided that I too, like the good knight, should reduce my library. It's hard to get rid of books. You can donate them to a church or a library, but really to get rid of books is an ethical problem, as one would have to rewrite them all. I still have more than eight books at home, but I am getting closer and closer to being Don Quixote's gentleman.

Here is an illustration of the kinetics of the machine. I must say that the *act* is the experience. The machine is not about the object, the object is just documented here – it's about the experience one has in participating in it. Of course, the act is different for the reader and for the voyeur, the onlooker, because the reader is involved in the undecipherable or in the completely transparent. But the voyeur, the one who looks on the reader, sees only a body bent over this wheel of torture, and he sees only a beautiful kinetic motion. When the wheels and the little gears move it's truly beautiful – the fascination of multiplying a circle. The experience one has is that the books on the top shelf, which are rotating, appear to be falling on top of you. This is what I was after. They appear to be falling on your head as you pull the wheel or as you read. It's a very uneasy feeling. And as you turn the wheel, the book which you've just left behind, which is going down, appears to be falling on to the ground. The books fall on your head and on the ground but, at the same time, never falling on your head and never falling on the ground; always remaining in the same position because the axle rotates very accurately, keeping them in an ideal position to a hypothetical reader – a reader who isn't there.

That's the reading experience: one cog of the entire machine. Not a starting point, but one element of the bigger machine. You will see it repeating itself in all the other machines.

Let me move on to remembering architecture. I've been told that when people die (and I've also read a lot about it), when one remembers one's life before committing suicide or when dying in a hospital, life reels rapidly in front of one's brain. And at the end things become quickly apparent. They very quickly pile up into the soul. In an end condition, then, things pile up rapidly in the memory of what architecture may have been. It's hard to know; but I set myself this task: to remember architecture, to construct an experimental being who could remember it. So lesson B is that which is no longer in the arena of craft, in the arena of this future past, but it's in the arena of future eternal, of ideas. So we came out of the monastery. We didn't do this one with the notion of pure life on our knees, with our bare hands, praying that someone should save us; but rather in an ideological realm of politics, a kind of Renaissance notion of architecture. It's really the monks coming with their weapons out of the monastery, and appearing on the stage of the theatre. Therefore, lesson B consists of that which can still be remembered of architecture.

As an historical programme, architecture and its sight have been filtered through what can still be remembered. I modelled this machine after a very fascinating phenomenon to me: a small memory machine constructed in sixteenth-century Venice by an architect called Giulio Camillo. Giulio Camillo was perhaps in his time the most famous architect and an opponent of Palladio in some ways. He was commissioned by the King of France to build a little machine which, in a split second, could reveal the meaning of the cosmos. I thought that was a worthy cause and a worthy memory. And apparently Giulio Camillo, the architect, fulfilled himself nobly. This comes to me from his correspondence with Erasmus, who has always been very truthful about everything. Giulio Camillo showed a small machine to the King of France in the sixteenth century. The King walked up to it (it was a small object, obviously), looked into it, turned around and said to Camillo: 'Now I understand. I understand everything. You are an architect. You have revealed to me the meaning of it all.' The interesting thing about Camillo is that immediately after he made this machine, two things happened: the machine disappeared and so did Camillo.

Ever since I read about Camillo's machine I have been absolutely enthralled by it. I wanted to meet Camillo, and I wanted to know more about it because I'm also trying to remember what it used to be like, as he did. I went to London and discovered Frances Yeats who wrote a book on Camillo, and I found that nothing more is known about Camillo's theatre than what was written in her book: that it was made out of wood, had paper which was hanging, and had rope in it. Those are the only absolutely objective facts about it: rope, hanging paper and wood. I tried in the presence of these ideas to remember through Camillo's mind: architecture.

I have designed only the backstage of Camillo's mechanism here as a model of the mind of the Renaissance in which equipment and architecture first comes to its own manifestations. The theatre, this little machine, is very, very simple. It's made from many pieces of wood, paper and string, constituting the source of illusions of some olympic theatre. The first machine with the books is already here in this machine inside the wood. I should say that the sound is very important because the sound of equipment is important, and this is a piece of equipment to be used. The first piece of equipment was creaking; this machine clicks like a puppet theatre. You can use it, manipulate it, pull the strings. I guess it's a little puppet of memory – a theatre of architecture, rather than the architecture of a theatre. And this too I read in *Don Quixote*. You might recall that there was a puppet show that he once saw somewhere in Spain. The King was vilifying the maiden and Don Quixote, being the good and noble knight, pulled out a sword and cut off the King's head. The poor puppeteer jumped out from behind and said: 'Hey, just a minute. This is not the real thing, this is only the play.' It was too late. Clearly Don Quixote de la Mancha could not tell the difference between the puppet and reality, the representation and its source.

I have to say now that none of these machines were invented by me. The whole process is to get oneself out of it. One has put oneself into it historically, but one must, at some point, disappear. Well, this is my way, my three stages of the way out. For Kirkegaard it was 'either/or', but this is a more ambiguous process of getting oneself out. You can say out of the object and into the experience; out of the inanimate into the spiritual; out of the non-being into being. What I tried to do with the problem of architecture, to put it another way, was to disengage it from its position on the earth. I was given a site in Venice and rather than doing what I think most architects are doing today, which is to engage the problem of architecture in the earth, in its own soil, I tried to disengage the problem of architecture from the earth – to send it into its stellar source. There were two stars I sent it to – two places where it all came from, I think. One is east, one is west. I think in the west it came from Dublin. So I sent back all of this project – everything from Venice, from Venetto, from the Renaissance, from Palladio, Camillo – to Dublin c/o Mr Joyce. Because I said in my programme here that I would seek to release the end to itself. And on the other hand I sent it back to Moscow, c/o Mr Tatlin, because it also came from Moscow in some sense. Moscow and Dublin, two capitals, not of the nineteenth century; they are capitals of the early twenty-first. So I sent this odradek (called 'odradek' by Kafka and meaning in Czech 'not to give any advice') back on the Moscow/Dublin route.

There are other things in this small memory machine to remember. There are little horses, little cloud machines, little wave machines, all sorts of instruments, measuring devices, because you may recall that in the first experience (the reading machine), the measurement came straight out of faith. But in the realm of ideas the measurement is a political measurement. It comes from an intersubjective dialogue. The text is also obliterated in another way as is the writing of the text, which is of course accomplished by writing architecture. This architecture is spread out and diffused or sprayed in a different manner across the screen of perception. The machine contains in it, by the way, the hanging papers seen by the King of France. An attempt is made to fill up the soul with memory so that one would finally obliterate it altogether. After a while there's really nothing you can remember anymore, only the process of storage. One more thing: there was a spiritual friend of Giulio Camillo. You may have heard of Giordano Bruno, the philosopher and heretic, who was burned in Rome exactly in the year 1600. He was expounding Copernican theory all over Europe, but the church decided he was out. Bruno was a type of spiritual architect and said that all his life he had been doing architecture. Well, he never built a building – he had been building the cathedral inside himself. He said: 'They're not building them anymore outside, so I'm building it inside.' And just before he was burned at the stake he said: 'I've almost completed it. I've got it completely inside. It's not necessary for me to have it outside.' Well, not everybody's Giordano Bruno or Giulio Camillo, but one has to try. So to put everything inside, this is what it would feel like. It would be suspended over you; the suspension of architecture. It's not really grounding it at all. And I know how everybody wants to ground architecture and bring it back home with that misreading of Heidegger – to go back to the forest, to your little hut – but I think Heidegger was out of this world altogether, what with National Socialism, mythology, spirit and the black forest.

The first machine taught me how to make the wheel, then I had to make what is called the barrow. I tried to make a wheelbarrow – I had to remember how to make it. When you look at the twentieth century, you see a lot of architects photographed next to the wheelbarrow: Mies van der Rohe, Le Corbusier, Behrens. But it's not quite believable that they are using it, since they are always in a suit or something like that. There's a beautiful photograph of Behrens in his tie and vest and top hat next to the wheelbarrow. So, I said, if I'm going to practise architecture I've got to get next to a wheelbarrow and *move it*. But it's hard to move because it sways a lot (which is not really due to the weight). The problem with the wheelbarrow is that the stuff is so suspended in it that it is hard to propel in one direction. But this is the second part. It's a sort of ideological bequest, and I can show you how the wheel and the barrow are engaged in a slightly more sophisticated whole: the written part both play in those pieces. Writing the book itself, by moving the barrow. Now, lesson C. I call this the writing lesson; not just the writing of anything but the writing of architecture lesson. This one teaches the artless and the scienceless making of architecture. I showed you the signs, the craft and the art of architecture. Now I would like to make architecture without signs and without art. Clearly signs and art are only stages on the way. I think it was Nietzsche who said that not only are painting and music beautiful pieces of art, but also the Prussian Army or the Jesuit Order. He would have been absolutely delighted to see the modern industrial state. This machine is the industrial part. First was craft: the 'one alone', and in there were the 'many alone' to remember it. Now I speak from the point of view that being 'one alone' is not enough. Being 'many alone' is not enough. One has to enter the full working force of the many: to do architecture without signs, without art, the way one would produce a pair of shoes. Now that I live in Milan I see a lot of shoe production, and I know what makes a good shoemaker there: he knows how to put the nail in the right place. The difference between the great and the mediocre shoemaker is the position of the nail. And that's what I tried to do, by learning how to put a nail in without art and without science; in other words, to industrialise the process I've been describing, to industrialise the poetics of architecture and to offer architecture as a sacrifice to its own possibilities of making a text.

The writing machine processes both memory and reading materials and is a cybernetic hinge because now it's a matter of mounting the gear, the axle and the text into an industrial propulsion, and to do it experientially as an industrialist would. So first, one built by praying on one's knees – total faith. Second, one built by being politically astute, through measurement and discussion. The third step brings one to a nine-to-five job. I thought I needed more experience in the nine-to-five. Maybe one has been working nine-to-five all along but hasn't really got enough experience or participation in the process. So how does one get it? I think one opens a little business, a little industry. I got myself a clock with my friends – a time clock. We tried to reduce the problem to its bare minimum, technique, and not to make it interesting at all – to have all our fun after five. During the procedure we agreed to work hard, speak only in 'small talk', smoke cigarettes, dream about TV, but to try, in this project, not to contaminate it with other issues.

I started mounting the gear onto this prototype. You know that once you make one gear you get a little more confidence. You can make one which is slightly more complex. You can engage that gear not just with itself tautologically, but you can then project it along these axes, back and forward, and maybe somewhere altogether outside itself. I'd like to show you how it evolved. I built it out of wood. I continued with the gear. I opened a little factory making the little reading wheels. Then I used the books . . . I had to have a lubricant, fuel for the machine, and so I had to use the books. There had to be surfaces because it was not for one reader. To lubricate such a big industrial piece of writing one would need all the texts in the whole world, so I translated the books into forty-nine times four languages because seven words times seven is forty-nine cubes. The cubes are pinned on four sides revealing four faces which means forty-nine times four surfaces. Many, many axles to lubricate; many languages. The first machine creaks, the second one clicks, and this one, I can assure you, whirls rapidly. A very well-lubricated mechanism goes very, very fast – in any language. The books were then cut up slowly, and very particularly as the most poignant part of architecture is to use it all up. Because now one is making something that has to be useful, not just for those who are alone in the many, but to the many in one. I spliced the axles into intricate formations, like genetic codes, and all sorts of devices were invented in order to produce it.

Then came the problem of the housing unit – an architectural problem. This is an entry for an urban design competition. I had to deal with the dwelling units, economics, commerce, etc, which means I had to deal with the memory machine. But I had to reduce it to scale, so I reduced the memory machine with its little windows to this small artifact. Now I'll explain how it works conceptually and practically. The idea is this: to rotate *this* handle, but to move *that* far diagonal cube at a different rate from your rotation. So let's say you move it to the right once, and you move the diagonal cube to the left four times with that one movement. Or you rotate the right handle twice to the right and you move these four cubes here on the left three times forward. That's the complexity of the gear movement: it's all about technique. In reality that's what industrial modernity is all about; it is to engage those reading cycles and those memory wheels into a kind of securing or stock-taking which would yield unexpected results. It's primitive, but Pascal made his little calculator, and Babbage made his little computer, and, after all, the regular computers we have today are only based on two phases. They are so-called binary, black and white, which is what makes them so schizophrenic, because you always say either yes or no to everything, never maybe. I tried to make a quadripartite computer operation, which means to mirror the realm of decisions in a double of itself. One can say there are four parts. Perhaps they are the parts which belong to God and mortals, to the earth and to the sky. You can say they are the parts that belong to the four interchanges. So that's how I went about it with another prototype, in order to couple these configurations together into a rapid, whirling movement.

Now you can see the little swelling units, the little houses; you can see the roof gardens on top and that's the city itself, and at the back you see the big piston that goes up and down. By going up and down in the vertical it can turn it all. The horizontality can be transformed into the diagonal movement. Here is the kit which was manufactured for one cube. I didn't do it monastically because I realised that industry can rely on other industry, so one can get all industries to work together happily. The machine is very complex. It has 2,662 parts, most of them are mobile, so you don't see them, but everything – the text that you see on the bottom, the assembly of the machine, the mosaic of movement – is coupled. The first machine had one drawing, like the medieval masons who had only one drawing: the drawing of the circle. The second one had already two drawings. And this one has, once again, one drawing, but the drawing is more like a diagram than a drawing – it engages the binary computer system into the larger grid over there. I believe that the modern city has a good deal in common with military problems. The vulnerability of the modern city is closely tied with the invisibility of the threat to the city. I think when the walls came tumbling down in history and the city was revealed, it died, though it apparently continues to exist. And I've often thought that the relationship between military vulnerability and the entity of the city as a visible organism, cannot be perceived in a visual attitude. It has nothing to do with the eye, because it is really the problem of equivalence between this particular configuration of a star and another particular star in the middle. The one in the middle is perhaps Houston, or maybe Chicago, or any city which is a new, right-angled, orthogonal star. But both of these stars don't shine unless one introduces a matrix in the back of them.

In the end, it's a problem of equivalence. Balzac said to comprehend is to equalise. So to equalise is here the task. I think all of us are equalisers, but in the process of equalisation one also has ritual duties, primarily to protect the text. The problem is to protect the text. It's like the mezzuzah in the Jewish tradition: that sacred text, the scroll – a bit of the Torah – which is pinned to each doorway of a household which makes the threshold sacred. I've often wondered why in the Jewish tradition they have to have it. I understood it when I became an industrialist. In the process of sanctification one also destroys the text, and one is then responsible in every way – I don't know, responsible to someone, to God himself – for protecting it. Everything became a technical problem. I had to wrap up time itself with words. When you get this kind of density of the text you've got to wrap it up very well indeed. You can see that the little wheels when they are coupled together are more efficient. And you can see that it gets busy. It gets very busy and nine-to-five is not enough: there is overtime. Immediately there is overtime. You know when you stack up these equivalences you stack up the two attitudes. You stack up the whole ending to itself. You get the matrix as stockpile. And then, as you work on the housing, resources appear in these urns. They wind up in these small shrines, funerary urns, and then one has the ashes inside of them. It is a ritual object that I'm showing you. Not an old-fashioned and then one has the ashes inside of them. It is a ritual object that I'm showing you. Not an old-fashioned ritual object, because these little shrines' ashes are not blown to the wind, nor stored in a particular position; they are mounted on an axle to be rotated permanently.

The writing machine is a machine to write a single text. The single text which it seeks to write is a text that has already been written by a particular author of the twentieth century. It's a text by Raymond Roussel, a French writer who wrote a book called *Impressions of Africa*. What Raymond Roussel tried to do is present in the text an experience which could never be had, either historically or in the future. Many people were interested in Roussel. Picasso said that he painted because Raymond Roussel inspired him to paint. Duchamp, the antagonist to Picasso, said that his work was all a footnote to Roussel. Le Corbusier said that he did architecture because of Roussel. Giacometti said he became a sculptor because of Roussel. Proust said that Roussel was classical French literature. Cocteau said that he took opium because he read Roussel. I can enumerate the list on and on, with all the heroes that I've got. It's time to interpret Roussel's text, yet how to go about it since this text is made out of nothing? It's about experience that could never be had. For example, in Roussel, there are certain miraculous figures that appear and disappear. There is Mossem. I don't know where Mossem comes from, but Mossem is killed in Roussel's book by having a text burned on his feet. It's an experience which could not easily be had. But then I discovered that St Theodore of Constantinople in the seventh century was killed by burning an iambic text on to his forehead. So it began to make sense. Then I find Angelica who appeared in Roussel. Angelica with the grid, who was finally burned on a grid as St Donatella, at a particular date in the third century AD. Well, there are forty-nine empty boxes. They have to be filled with ashes of unknown saints. Fortunately, there is a book of saints which can link up the impression of Italy, the impression of what can be said to be the end with the 'Africa of the mind', a kind of uncolonised or about-to-be colonised last region. I would say that Roussel is great because he is the coloniser of the remote parts of the brain, which are just about to be imperialised. In any case, that sort of equipment is not easy to explain but is easy to use. It helps to position the city in a spaceless space.

I should probably say what the four sides of this machine – this calculator – are. It's a little computer I built. A calculator which is to prognosticate the written destiny of architecture. By becoming an operator you can stockpile information resourcefully, information which is linked with a prophesy made by Victor Hugo that architecture is doomed to die because of the text. Victor Hugo said that the book will kill the cathedral. So I tried to make this computer following Victor Hugo and Jonathan Swift's 'Voyage to Laputa' into a pragmatic reality. Therefore, the four sides of these funerary boxes contain the following: on the first side, the city which doesn't shine anymore, that star of Palmanova which doesn't shine anymore, intersected and congealed into the rectilinear star, let's say of Mies van der Rohe; the occult star of victory boogie-woogie; the white and black stars congealed into a singular star. That's one side of the dwelling unit. The second is just a piece of metal which is a reflection which shatters the mathematics of it. It's a kind of reflective order which disrupts the forty-nine times four sides. Side three consists of a geometric sign which is actually an architectural horoscope. I did horoscopes on all the positions of all the saints in all the spots of Palmanova in order to derive where to cut them up. One cannot cut them up arbitrarily; one has to study all the stars and horoscopes. And the fourth side is the enumeration of the forty-nine saints, the saints who are needed for the completion of the pilgrimage: the pilgrimage of Absolute Architecture.

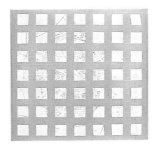

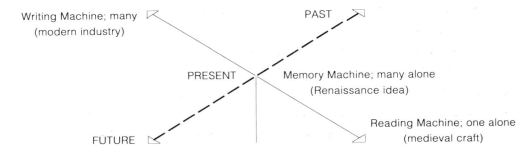

Writing Machine; many (modern industry)

PAST

PRESENT

Memory Machine; many alone (Renaissance idea)

Reading Machine; one alone (medieval craft)

FUTURE

reat ed bei ngc reate.

Dbe. I. Ngcreat, edbeingc reat edb eingcr ea ted beingcr ea

te dbeingcr. Eatedbein gc rea tedbe in gcr eate db eingcreat e

dbe ingcre ate dbeingc, re at ed beingcre, atedb ei ngcreate db Eingcreat. edb eing crea ted beingcrea *(ted bei.* N) "gcr eat e dbe ingc re at e dbeingc, re atedbe in **Teaches an almost forgotten (medieval) process of building, a process which is in its own way not yet fully unfolded in Architecture. Like the medieval monastery out of which the Reading Machine (dedicated to Petrarch) emerged, the method of construction and the technique of understanding bring about a revolution of architecture's techne which coincides with the movement of the text that it propels. As a place of intersection between archaeological reconstruction (Ramelli, Palmanova, military engineering) and the will to power it discloses (metaphysics, monasticism, ideology) the Reading Machine reveals the tautological reality of the architectural text. The eight Books – each a single word uttered by the forgetfulness of Being that resolves itself by turning back in order to come forward – lie on eight shelves. The Books come and go for a comparison not only with each other but with the weight of the last seven words of Metaphysics, which crush the gears and axels whose relation is inaccessible from the reading position. The wheel revolves, and in completing a revolution returns to its starting point while exposing its own uselessness and kinetic beauty.**

Executed in a 'medieval' manner, with glueless joints and using no energy of a contemporary kind, this machine represents the triumph of spirit over matter; of candle light over darkness. It is made solely from wood, as are the books.

gcrea, te dbe ingcr eated be, in createdb, ein gc r eated; bei ngcreate db ei, ngcr eat edb

ein cre atedbei ng creat ed be, ingcrea ted bein gcr eate dbe in

gc reate dbeing" *(CrEate.* db, E)

Dbe. I. Ngcreat, e dbeing crea tedbei ng c reatedb. Ein gcr

eate db e ingcre ated, being cr ea ted

ENERGIA

IAENER G. *I Aener*

ener. Giaen erg IAENE RGIAENE,

rgiaene RGIAEN.

Iaene. Rgi, aen erg, Iaener! gia ener
  giaener.

ia. Ener G iae nergia, energia en erg iae,
  gi aen ergiaene? Rgi aen erg iaen

e nergia ene rgiaenergi aenerg.

ner gia ene; rgia energ I'ae rgiae
g i aenerg iae n ergia ene;
ae nergiaen ergi ae nergiae ner giae.
g iae nergia en erg iaen
ia energ i aenergia ener giaenerg;
 nergi ae ner gi aene rg iaener;
 ener giaene'r gi aener giaenerg
ne rgiae nerg iaenergiae nergiae
g iae nergiaen er giaen ergiaener
en ergi aen er gi aen ergiaener.
 ener giaen ergi, aener giaen, erg iaen

CREAT EDBE I. NG. CRE. A

creat edb eingcreate db ein gcre,'' atedbeing cr eat Edbeingc.
Reatedbei ngc reat ed bei ngc reate.

Dbe. I. Ngcreat, edbeingc reat edb eingcr ea ted beingcr ea
te dbeingcr. Eatedbein gc rea tedbe in gcr eate db eingcreat e
dbe ingcre ate dbeingc, re at ed beingcre, atedb ei ngcreate db

cre ated b eing cr ea tedbei ng cr eatedb.

Eingc Rea. T. Edbe in gcr eatedb ei ngc reat edb ei ng create
dbe in gc reatedb ein gcreat edbeingc re ate dbei, ngcrea, ted
beingcrea ted bei ngcr; eat ed being create dbe ing crea te db e
ingc re ate dbei. Ngcre atedbe ing create db ein gcre ate dbei.
Ngcreated bein gc reate dbeing crea ted be ingcreat edb eing c
rea, tedb ei ngcr eate db ein gcre atedb ei ngcreatedbei ng cre
atedbeing cr eate d being.

ROWE. RP. *Owerpow erpowerp ow erp owerpower po
werp, owerp owerpowerp, ower po we rpo, werpowerp
werp owerp owerpow.*

Erpower. Power po werpowe rpowerpo we rpowe
po werpowerpo w erpo we rpowerp (Ower. PO, we. R).

erpo werp owerp ower po werpo, wer power powe rp ow
er po werpo, wer po *we rpowerpow.* Erp ower po werp
w erpowerpow.

ERPO. WE. *Rpo werpo werp owe rpow erpowerpo we
power po wer powe, rpo werp owe rpowe rp owerp owe*

Rpowerp. Owe rpowe rp owe rpowe rp owerpowe.
po we Rpo wer pow erpower po Wer po wer powe rpo w
erpo werpowerpo we rpowerpowe. Rpow er powerpowe

Spirits pir Itspi Rits

(Pirit spi Ritsp irits.)

PIRIT. Spiri tspi rit spi rit spiritsp irits,
Piritsp ir it spi Ritspi'r itsp-iritsp iritspi
Ritsp iri tspiri tspirit spi ritsp,
Iritspi rit spirit's pirit spiritsp.
Iritspir itspir itspiri tspi
Rits pi rit spirit spiritsp iritsp;
Irits, pirit spiritspir, itspir itspi,
Rit spirit spiritspir itspiri tspiri, -
Tspirits pir it Spiri't spirits.

SUBJECTSUBJ

SUBJECTSUBJEC

ects ub jectsubjec ts ubjectsub je cts ubject su bj ect s
b jects ub jec tsub je ct sub ject subj ectsubjects ub je
: tsubj, ect subj ec tsu bjectsubje ct su bj ec. (Tsubjec

ectsu bjec ts ubject su bjectsub jec tsubjectsu bj ectsu
bjec tsubject su b jects ub jec tsubject ts ubje ctsubject
subjectsubj, ec tsu bjec tsubject tsub.
tsu bjectsu ts ubjects ub j ectsu bjectsubj ec tsubjectsu, bj
ct sub jectsu bjectsub jectsu bject sub ject su b jects u
bje; cts ubje ctsu bjectsubje ctsu, bj ect subject su b jec
subj, ectsubje ct subjectsub jectsubjec ts ubjec tsubjec
: tsu bjectsu bj e ctsub jectsubject subject, subject sub

Spir its piri tspiri't spiritspir itsp.
Irit spi rits piritspi ri tsp irits.
Pir, its pir itspir its pirits pirits
Pir itspir its pi ritsp iri tsp;
Iri tsp iri tspir itspi rit spiri
Tspi rit spiri tspir its pir,
Itspi rits pir itspiri tspir, its pirits
Pir itsp-irits pirit spir.
Itsp iri tspirit spiritsp irits
Piritsp iri tspir it spirit spir.

WILLTO POWE RWILLTO

POW.

Erw illtopow erwilltop O werw illto: "*Powe rw illtopowe r will t'opo w'erw, ill topowerwi ll topow.*"

ERW.

Ill topowe rwill topo we rwil lt opowerwill topo werw il
powe rwill topowe rw il. L topowerwillt opower wil ltopow er w

Llto po wer willtopowe *rwilltop*, owe, rwilltopower, wil lto
powe: *rwillt opowerw i llto powerwi llto powerwil.* Ltopower
Wil. LT.

OPO.

We rwillt opowe rwilltop ower willtopo werw il ltop, owe r
wil lt opowerw illtopower wi llto powerwil lt opowe rwilltop: ow
erw illtopo werwi ll topo werw i lltop?

B. E. I N.

BEINGBE, BEI NG, BE

POW.		B.E.I.N.				
BEi	NGb	EinGbeing	BEIN	GBe	INg	BEi-
GB	Ei	NgbeI n	GB	EIn		GBe
INg	BEi	NgbeI	NG	BEi	NG	BEi +
GBe	INg	Beingb	EI	NGb	EIn	GBe +
Ng	Be	Ingbei	NG	BEi	Ng	Be-
NGb	Ei	Ngbein	GBEI	NGb	EIn	GBe +
NGb	Ei	Ngbein	GB	EIn	GBe	INg-

BE	I	Ngbeln g	BEI	N	Gb	E
INg	BE	IngbeiN	GB	EIn	GBe	INg +
EIn	GBe	Ingbe i	NG	BRi	NGb	EIn
GBe	In	GbEing	B	EIn	GB	EIn
GBe	IN	GbeiNg	BEI	NG	BEi	NGb
Gb	Ei	Ngbein	GBE	In	Gb	Ei-
GB	EIn	Gbeing	BEI	NG	BEi	NG +
Ei	Ng	BeIngb	EI	N	Gb	E +
NGb	EIn	GbeiNgb	EI	NG	BEi	NG +
EIn	GBe	IngBei	NG	BEi	NGb	EI +
Gb	Ei	NgbeIn	GB	Ei	Ng	Be

be, in createdb, ein gc r eated; bei ngcreate
db ei, ngcr eat edb

ein cre atedbei ng creat ed be, ingcrea ted
bein gcr eate dbe in

Consists of that which can still be remembered in Architecture. As an historical programme the sites have been filtered through Giulio Camillo's Memory Theatre. As a precise weaving of the memory tradition with the agony of a 'Deus ex machina' this theatre represents the workings of a Renaissance Mind and shows its internal equipment and the arrangement it reveals.

The Memory Machine (dedicated to Erasmus) consists of the backstage only – the spectacle takes place wholly outside of it. As a mechanism for projection, concealment and illusion, this prosthetic piece of equipment exposes and also hides the Venetian projects.

Since the process of its construction remains in the classical arena (imagination, measurement, idea) the subversive element of mechanics (Teatro Farnese versus Teatro Olimpico) enters only in those places where memory has succeeded in retaining its surrogate authority.

As a ghost of Humanism's cosmic hubris, the Memory Machine seeks to disengage the sites from the earth in order to return them to their original, destined locus: Joyce's Dublin and Tatlin's Moscow.

Done in a 'Renaissance' style of being, the Memory Machine abounds in the kind of inventiveness and caprice that we associate with the Odradek.

It is executed in wood and retains in its structure the 'hanging papers' seen by the King. This project represents the stage of Architecture's appearance and is a testament to its own manifestation. Made of wood also are the eighteen subordinate spectacles, which include the 'cloud machine' as well as the 'schizophrenic forum'. Colourless: the bloody red illuminates the shiny exterior of an inner sanctum dedicated to what remains nameless. Metal is used exclusively for non-structural reasons, related as it is to light itself. Ropes are used throughout.

gc reate dbeing" *(CrEate.* db, E)

Dbe. I. Ngcreat, e dbeing crea tedbei ng c reatedb. Ein gcr

eate db e ingcre ated being cr ea ted

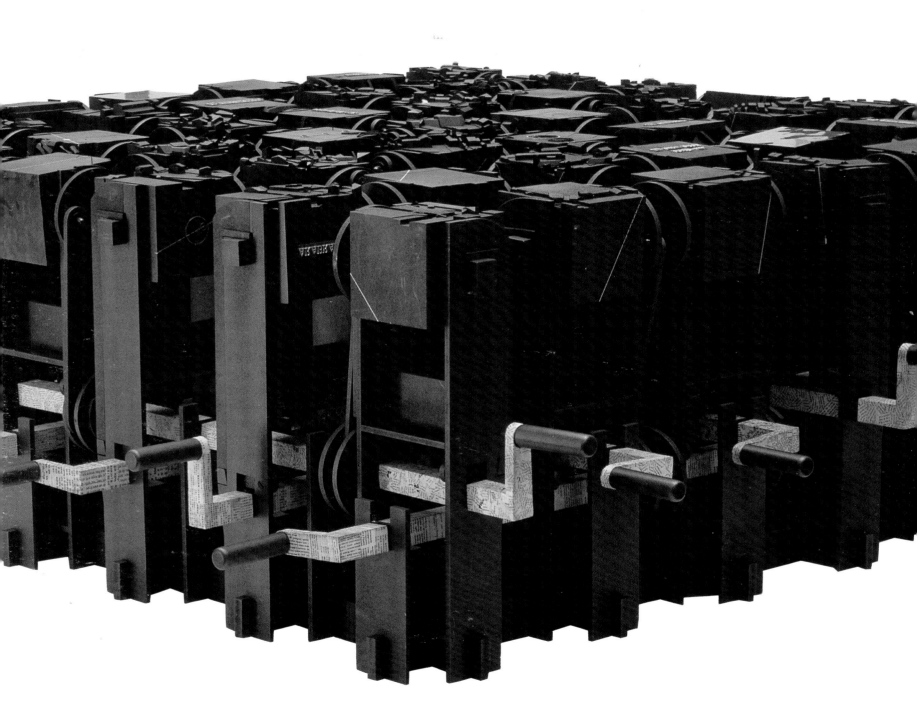

Teaches the artless and scienceless making of Architecture. As a fully engaged project, this machine industrialises the poetics of Architecture and offers it as a sacrifice to its own possibilities of making a text. Architecture, like shoemaking, becomes a problem of putting the nail in the right place.

Since the Writing Machine (which is black and throws a gleam dedicated to Voltaire) processes both memory and reading material, it takes what is projected into an exact account. Not only the City itself (Palmanova) but all places written into the book of Culture are here collected and disposed.

Through an enlightened vision the random mosaic of knowledge is gathered together into seven times seven faces, each mirrored in a quadripartite realm. The totality of Architecture is shattered by the foursome reciprocity of earth, sky, mortals and gods and lies open to a contemporary stocktaking.

The four sides of this 'Orphic' calculator or probability computer prognosticate the written destiny of Architecture whose oblivion is closely associated with Victor Hugo's prophecy. The four-sided cubes work in the following Swiftian manner:

Side 1: the City as a Star of Redemption is refracted and congeals into a 'boogie-woogie' constellation.

Side 2: is a metallic reflection which shatters and disrupts the spatial-mathematical order of the 49x4 sides.

Side 3: consists of a geometric sign which points to a graphic omen or architectural horoscope.

Side 4: enumerates the forty-nine saints who accompany the detached pilgrim in order to care for his unerasable vulnerability.

Thus the oppositions and complementary reciprocities which glide through the whole constitute a 'destabilised technology' which would break up the mechanism instantly if the computerised controls (twenty-eight handles) weren't there to keep it stable.

The Writing Machine is the first totally

te dbeingcr. Eatedbein gc rea tedbe in gcr
eate db eingcreat e

Dbe. I. Ngcreat, edbeingc reat edb eingcr

unstable text. As opposed to 'stable' architectural texts which best fly in a straight line of myth and resist the pilot's effort to climb, bank or dive, this 'unstable' prototype is extremely agile – having no natural flight path.

It jumps around the text's sky and is guided by an 'active control system' which can perhaps never again disclose its starting position (see position at the beginning, and position at the end). The Writing Machine is a contribution to Roussel scholarship. It links Africa and the Impressions of Italy through those miraculous figures whose presence is both inevitable and contingent. Angelica, with a grid, burnt on a grid: St Donatella; Mossem, killed by burning of text on to feet, killed by burning Iambic text onto forehead: St Theodore of Constantinople. By rotating the 'foursome', the arrangements appear ready for interpretation. These seemingly random relations are generated by an extremely sophisticated system which consists of 2,662 parts, most of them mobile. All are involved in an unpredictable rationalisation of place, name, person. Once in motion, the stockpiling and accounting of places, cities, types of buildings, gods, signs, saints, imaginary beings, forgotten realities, will present almost insurmountable difficulties for the operator, yet these are difficulties which can be eliminated through the revolutionary discipline of this turn towards a Budddhism of Action.

The machine is made of wood, graphite and metal and contains:

1) complex gear-shaft driven systems which rotate the multi-lingual papers;

2) forty-nine cubes which revolve at various speed ratios;

3) faces which show:

a) Euro-African City

b) Saints who have emerged from the project and who return to Roussel's Book of Saints

c) the empty Sky;

4) divined graphic configurations based on horoscopes and omens.

ea ted beingcr ea

te dbeingcr. Eatedbein gc rea tedbe in gcr

eate db eingcreat e

dbe ingcrea ate db eingcr ue at ed beingcrea

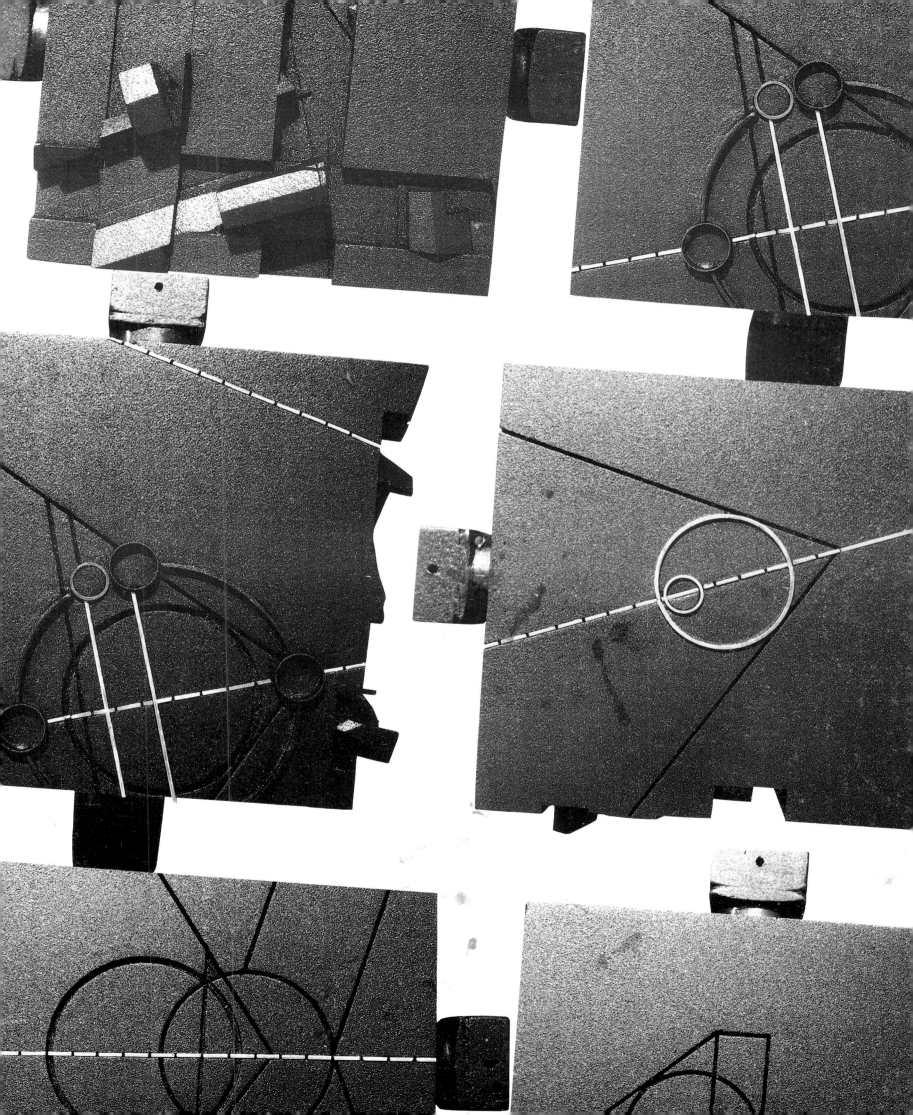

ROWE. RP. Owerpow erpowern ow erp owerpower po werpo
werp, owerp ow 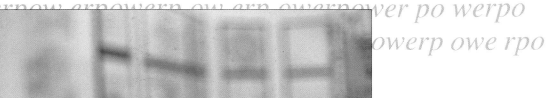 owerp owe rpo
werp owerp ow

  Erpower. Pow   owe rpowe r
po werpowerp   we. R) . Pow ep
owerp owerpo   w (erp ow erp o
wer power pow   er); pow erp o
werpower po w   werpowe rpow
erpow, er pow erpo werpower, pow erpo we rpo werp ower po

werpow erpo wer powern owe rpow erpowe rp owe rpow erpo
we rpo werp o   .P.O.
  Werpo. Werp  ow erpo w
erp owerpow e   verpower po W
erp. O, we. R, p   r powe rp ower
powe rpo wer   ow. E), rpo we
rp owe rpo we   erpo werpo we
rpo werp ow e   po werpowe, r
po we rpowerp owerp ower po werpowerp. ower pow er pow er

po, werpowerp owe rpo wern owerpo wer pow erp owe rpow er
pow, erpow er   rpow erpowerp
po, werp ow er   wer powe rp o
we rpow erp o   pow epo werp o
werpower pow   w. Erp, owerp
o, wer powe rp   werp ow erp ow
er, po werpowe   wer po werp o
wepowerpow e   e rpowerpo we
rpo werpow, erpo we r powerpow owe rpowe rpowerpo, we rpow

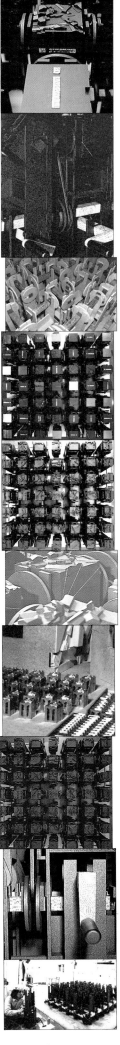

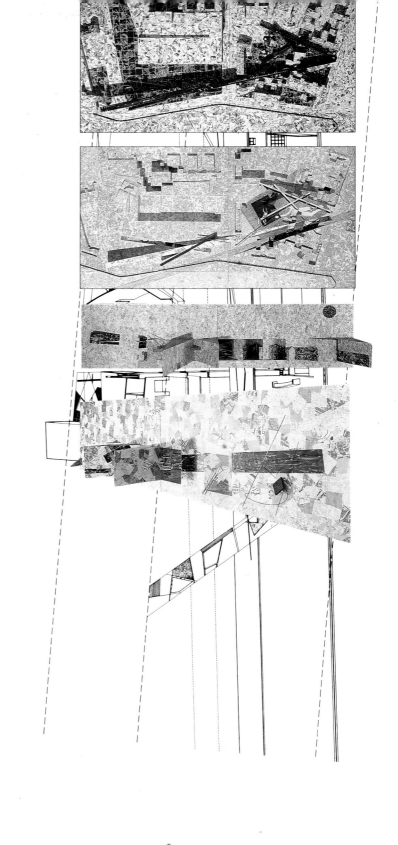

BERLIN 'CITY EDGE', 1987

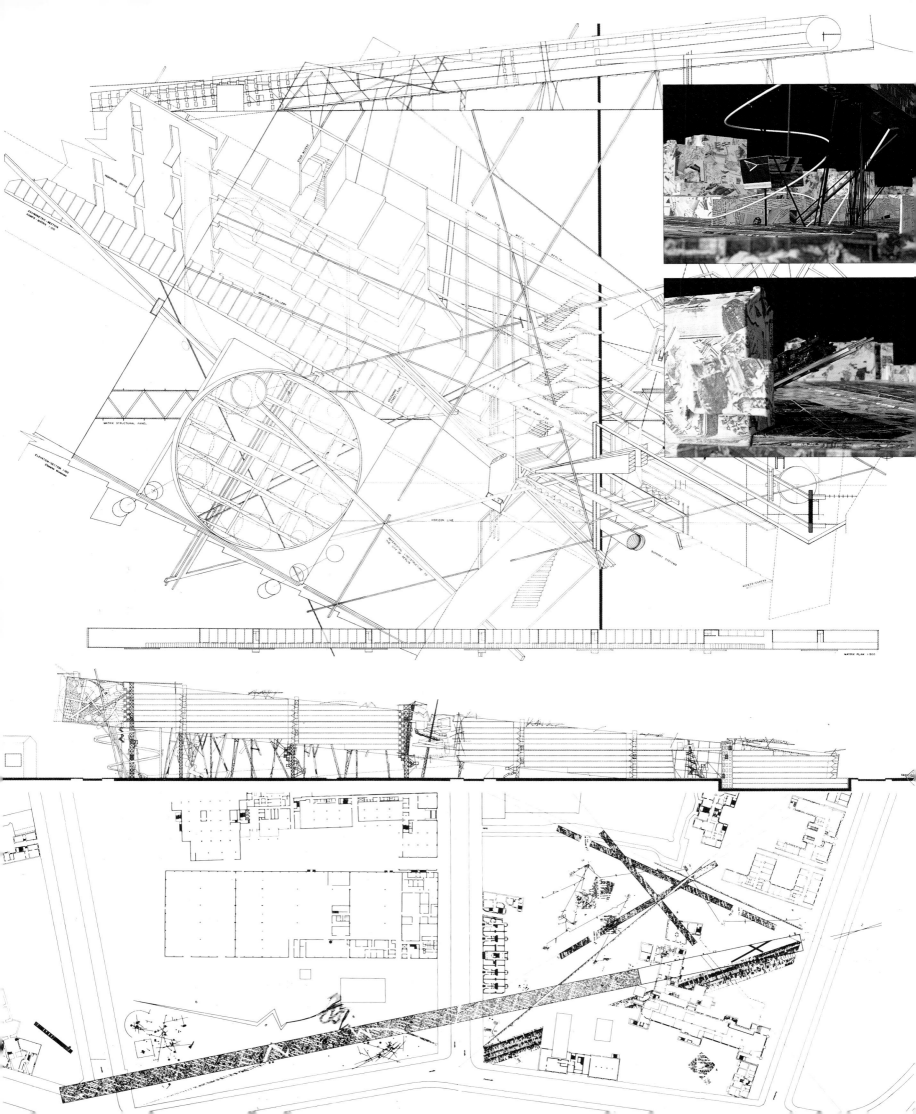

The building as a 'city-edge' emerges along the Flottwellstrasse and gives a view of the park along its entire edge, while simultaneously unifying Block 228/240 into an urban structure for dwelling, commerce and public activity.

The project seeks to demonstrate, in terms of planning, the possibility of utilising the traditional block structure of Berlin, while at the same time transcending its physical limitations. The aim is to create a new scale and a new type of living for the Berlin of tomorrow. The building is organised around a pedestrian boulevard which provides along its entire length for the transformation of experience from the boulevard of yesterday to the city structure of tomorrow.

Ancient vistas of cities and buildings, like memorable places and names, can be found on maps – the books of the world. Each appears in a different colour on a different background, though any colour can be exchanged for another by a traveller whose destination is not found on the map.

A voyage into the substance of a city and its architecture entails a realignment of arbitrary points, disconnected lines and names out of place along the axis of Universal Hope. Very thin paper – like that of architectural drawings, Bibles, maps, telephone books, money – can be easily cut, crumpled or folded around this indestructible kernel. Then the entire unwieldy construction can be floated on water like the tattered paper making its Odyssey on the Liffey. Finally the water itself can be adhered to the mind, provided that one does not rely on the glue. In this way Reality, as the substance of things hoped for, becomes a proof of invisible joys – Berlin of open skies.

In exploring the shape of this sky which continually refuses to come into identity or equivalence, one discovers that what has been marked, fixed and measured nevertheless lapses in both the dimension of the indeterminate and the spherical. This space of non-equilibrium, from which freedom eternally departs and towards which it moves without homecoming, constitutes a place in which architecture comes upon itself as beginning at the end.

1 Erased line: Historical Axis. A public space: Edge, limit, delusion. Speer's ordered disorder. Underneath the ground the city traces its own schizoid memory and protects it by insulating and covering the site. What is unforgotten cannot be eradicated, concealed. Opening unbuildable realms which stretch directly into the foundations, the block discloses a public space. By cutting off the presence of fragments, both the street and the area of building is reconsecrated. Reconstructing that which cannot be filled up, the site abruptly turns its own emptiness into an Archimedian point.

2 The Fulcrum: 24 Am Karlsbad. A monument in the park: A turning point. Crisis towards which possibilities return in order to revolve an invisible lever. Proposal for the Fulcrum of Universal Ideals. Chiasm of direction whereby an X grounds itself in the sky. Mies van der Rohe hanging pieces of glass outside of his window in order to study their reflections.

3 Solid line: Dwelling in its totality. Housing, offices, public administration: Building as crossing the site, blocking the historical (always ready to leap again . . .), cutting the remaining fragments, unhinging the horizon. Re-establishment of a City without Illusion, an architecture without limits. To realign the sky against diagonal intersections: the ground-prop instead of a sky-hook. By opening the space between the fulcrum and its virtual arc, the solid line grounds itself in the sky. Now the unsupportable supports the support: new techniques at ground level. Intermingling of life and work by retrieving Utopia from the pit.

4 The Field: Intersecting nature. A Garden in the City: The spared preserves what is to come. Four quarters of the ancient sky reflected upon the Earth establish common points: necessity in contingency, chance in axioms. The framing of variety cinematically suspended in an acrobat's leap.

5 The Throw: Child's Play. Children's Day Facility: Reorienting the site towards its own play of place. A child's hope as a way of knowing and ordering the site across lines which cut themselves off from the web. Paths across and out of the block. Buildings whose vectors emerge, criss-cross and roll on the ground.

6 Compressing curves into straight lines. Commerce, Industry: The space production. Imploding a curve into an angle – horizontally.

7 A final point: The beginning of a new diagonal: Moving out of dark crevices and corners. Walter Benjamin's unexpected encounter with the locomotive in the clouds.

Ts ubj ects ub jectsubjec ts ubjectsub je cts ubject su bj ect s
bject su b jects ub jec tsub je ct sub ject subj ectsubjects ub je
t su bjec tsubj, ect subj ec tsu bj ectsubje ct su bj ec. (Tsubjec
ub JE.)

Cts ubjectsubjectsubje ct subjectsub je cts ubject su bj ect s
bje ... Subje C.).

Tsu ... ubj ec tsub ject subjectsu bjectsubj ec ts
Ubj

Cts ... e ctsu bj ects ub jects U bjec tsu bj ec
... ubject; sub jec tsubjectsu bje ct subj
... ct sub ject su
bj ectsu b

STILL LIFE WITH RED PREDICTIONS

Letalin will fly back, without Ulalume. Sharp staccato sounds will bypass Cerebrus barking, *sui juris*, at the stranger in us; will be transmitted by heredity to the abracadabra violoncello playing a solo motet in slow neon without the bow, without the cello.

Odours creating the illusion of rotating, difficult to taste conventions will ripple the water already agitated by a continual barrage of ancient texts thrown into it. Both odour and water will become things permanently verging on spinning, like the Ring. A similar example in metal: wilful arcs of polished motel siding fused with astral fibres will be used for making the discus or shield protecting local poverty from being beaten up by an alien ratio.

One will acquire a funny hypnotic power over flattened minds, particularly those of stupid museum curators who reject ornithological art because it is influenced by Chopin's flighty spirit. One will censor the invisible writings by General Pétain which hide in the delicate Art Nouveau ornament of the Métropolitain – provided one is willing to reconnoitre a flat cladophyll with a feeling of remorse.

Inside each piece of furniture – even tall ones – there will be a play performed. A delicate young lad in the dead of winter will be able to participate in a sensory-ritual quest for lost birch, pine and linden trees now replaced by single-fit smells of ionisation exclusively designed to furnish each living room with rapid, national bursts of sneezing. Tulips anyone?

Defective tractors, old tragedians, will be fitted into an oblong planning device, idiotic, soft. The suggestion that 'lately the future is appealing only to actors who can kill their audience without a licence' will become a source of inspiration to many. Farming will be illegal, pleasant.

(Ibn in Arabic, Ben in Hebrew, and so on.) Preface the lament with Beelzebub's concern for spicy Amontillado, a phenomenal offer. Tip. Mme Sevigny, in flight a chevron, plummets with great velocity towards Hotel Murillo, Unter den

Linden 1762, Berlin. Tip. And even more. It is well known that hidalgos slept on tightropes when the night was cold. Certain snoring sounds were labelled as repulsive when their musculature contracted to a sixth of its size with the sound 'shhhh . . .' – fickle power when tacitly negotiating for deep sleep with an owl! Vishnu, called the Preserver, believed that popular tradition had an odd number of knees – demanded that the sempiternal drip through a sieve without tying the carcass to an incarnation on wheels or increasing timidity enormously. The body's largest arrested organ: skin.

Indigence, an advantage without talent. The Sphinx killed herself though the deception perpetrated was half human, half Nordic or the sculptor's mumbo-jumbo. Must every fault be brought to silence by solitude? Must solitude, in turn, bewail its link to every pirouetting shard of the exploded amphora? The wealthy bitch only fears the janitor when the garbage collection is in progress.

The last letter of the first story must have been the first letter of the last story since Egyptians spoke a Hebrew dialect whenever they inserted a scarab into their mouth to simulate a circumcision best performed in secret. The rage for randomly selected victims has softened those who are still lingering in bed.

Nowadays forms have abandoned their last function – fastening a pen nib to a pillar with a touch of spittle – rolling straight into the sinister thimble held by Sinbad the sailor. Who will decipher, save and entertain purple hostility? Poems will be readily available if you call the right number or pull the lip all the way down till it touches the element. Fencing will become a fashionable sport. Dangling in a loophole will seem as interesting as artificial onions which sprout in the museum's seawater. Skin stretches to allow a couple of others in without discomfort thus disproving that incarnation alone is capable of emptying the destination of its meaning. Anyone can fit into an imaginary three-dimensional envelope provided one is hollow, ie, fully two-directional.

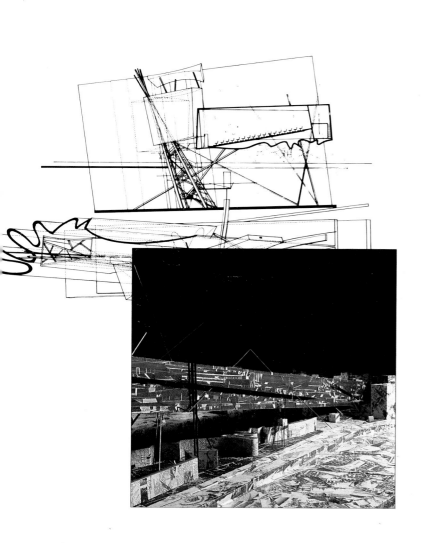

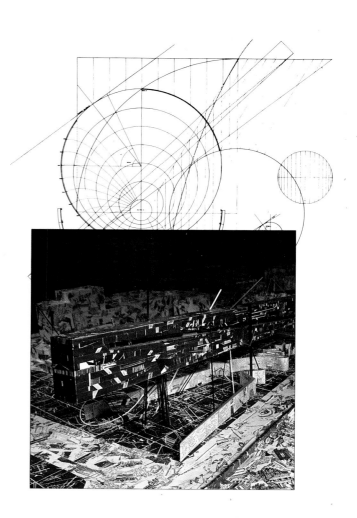

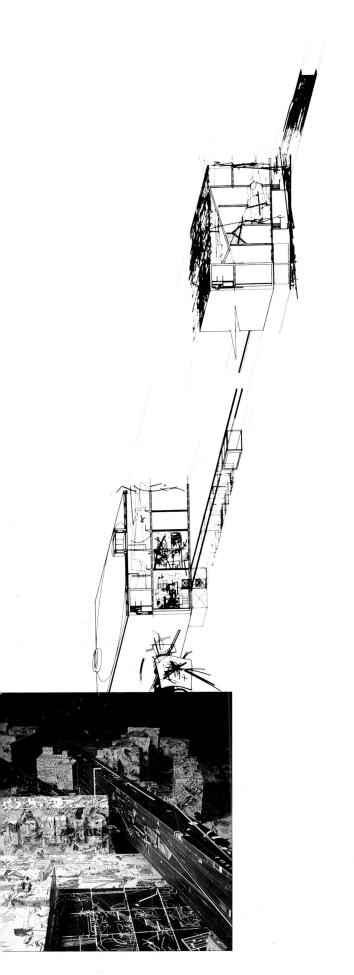
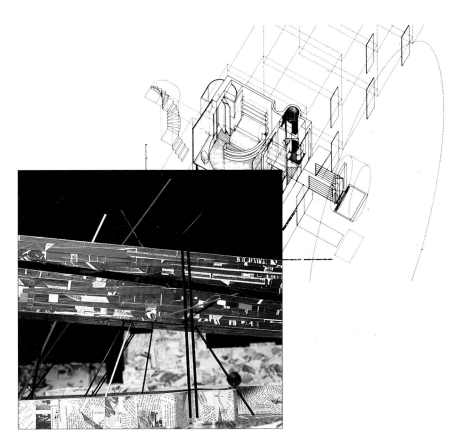

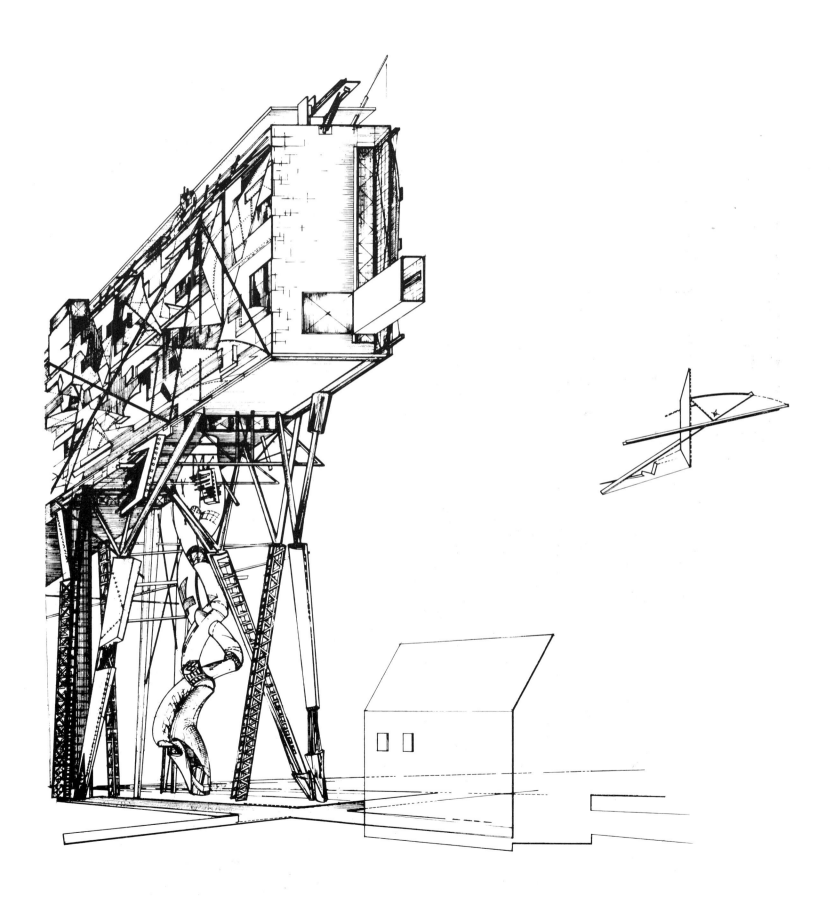

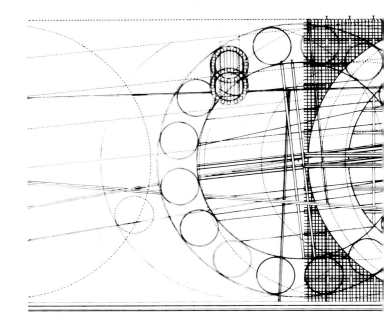

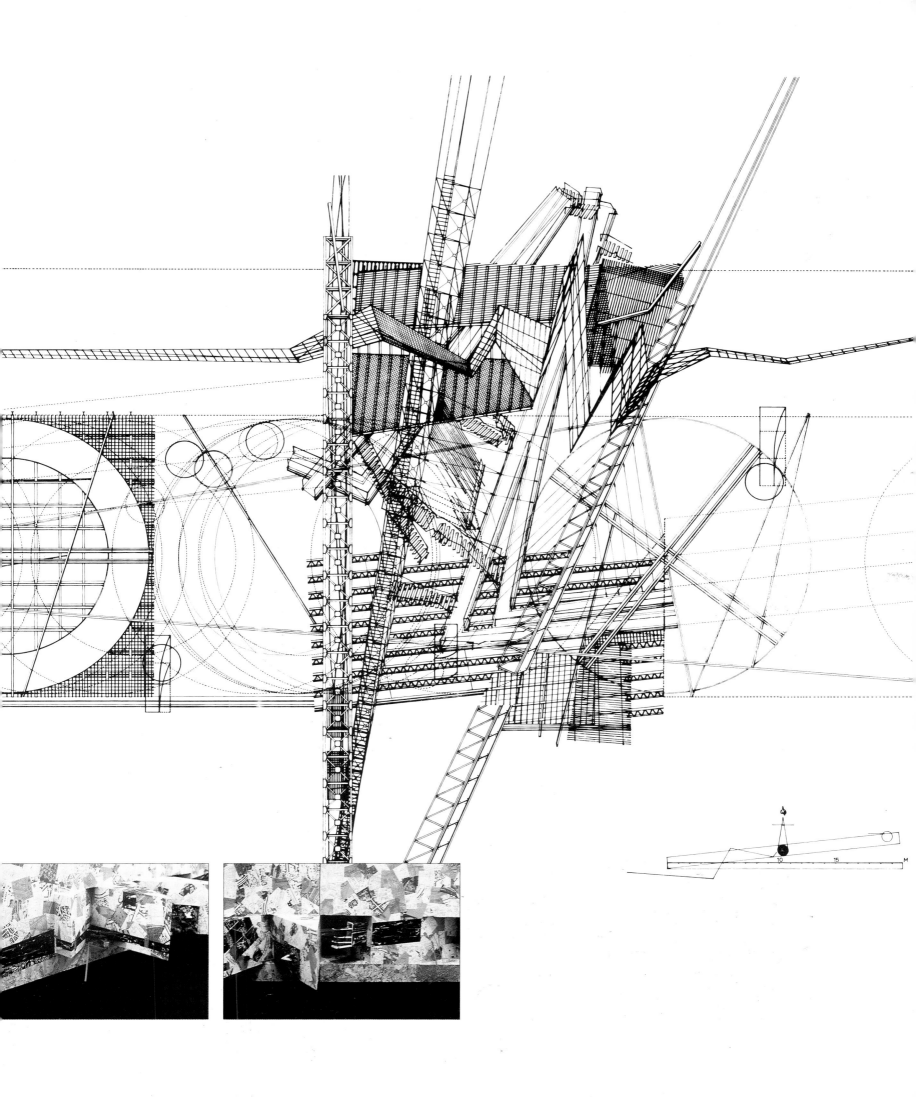

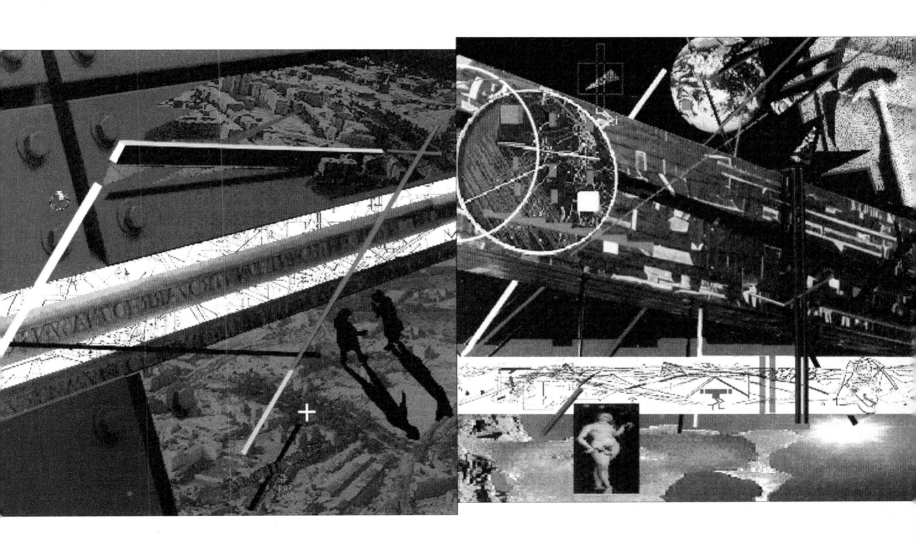

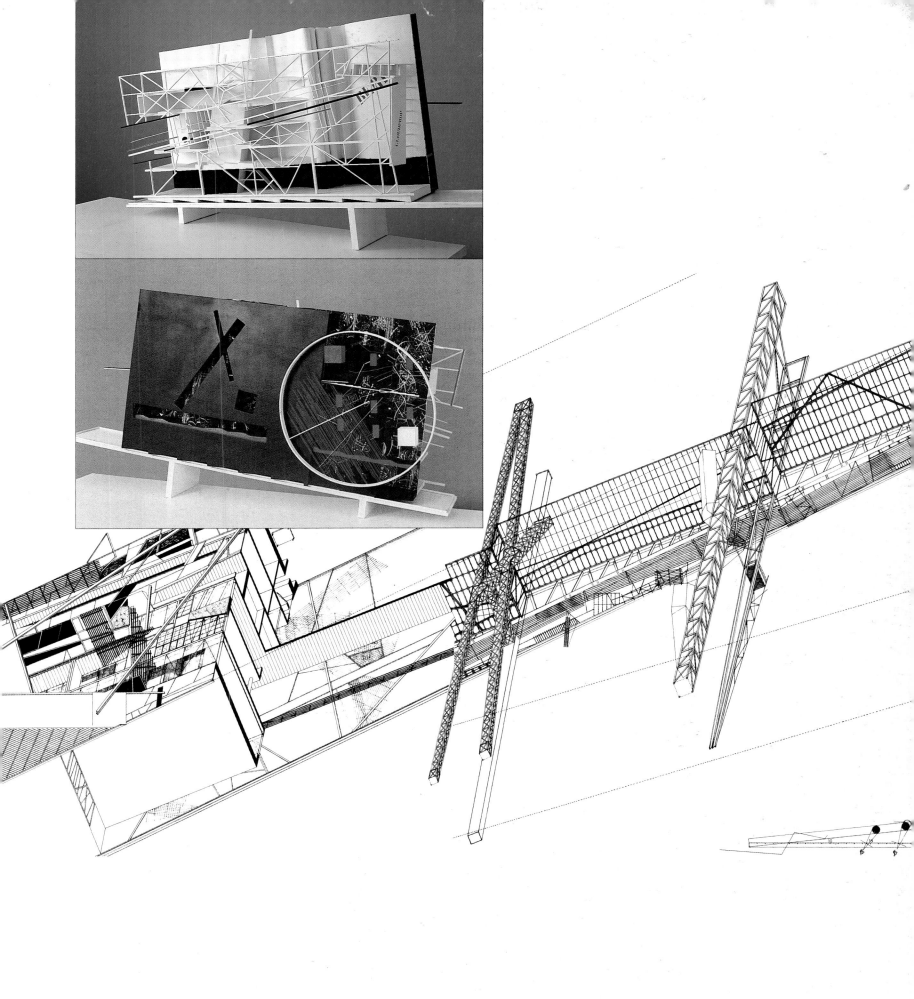

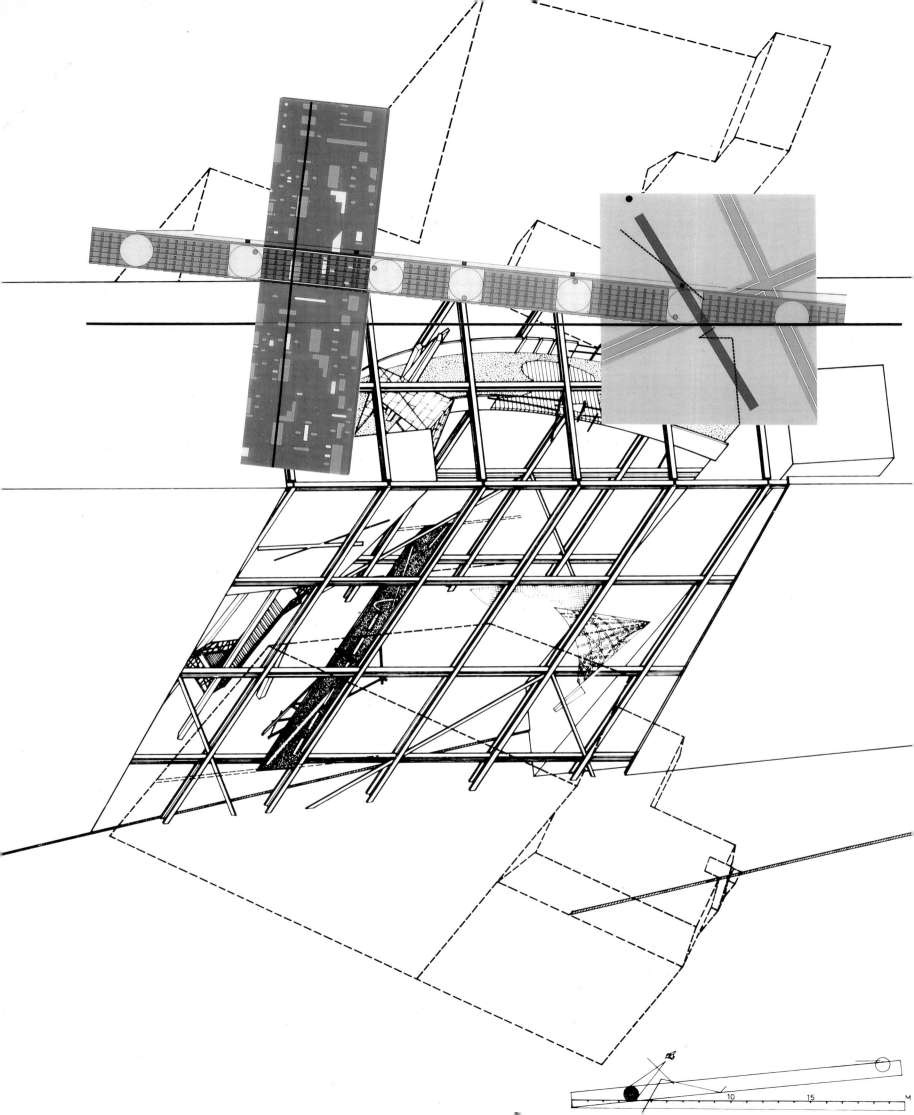

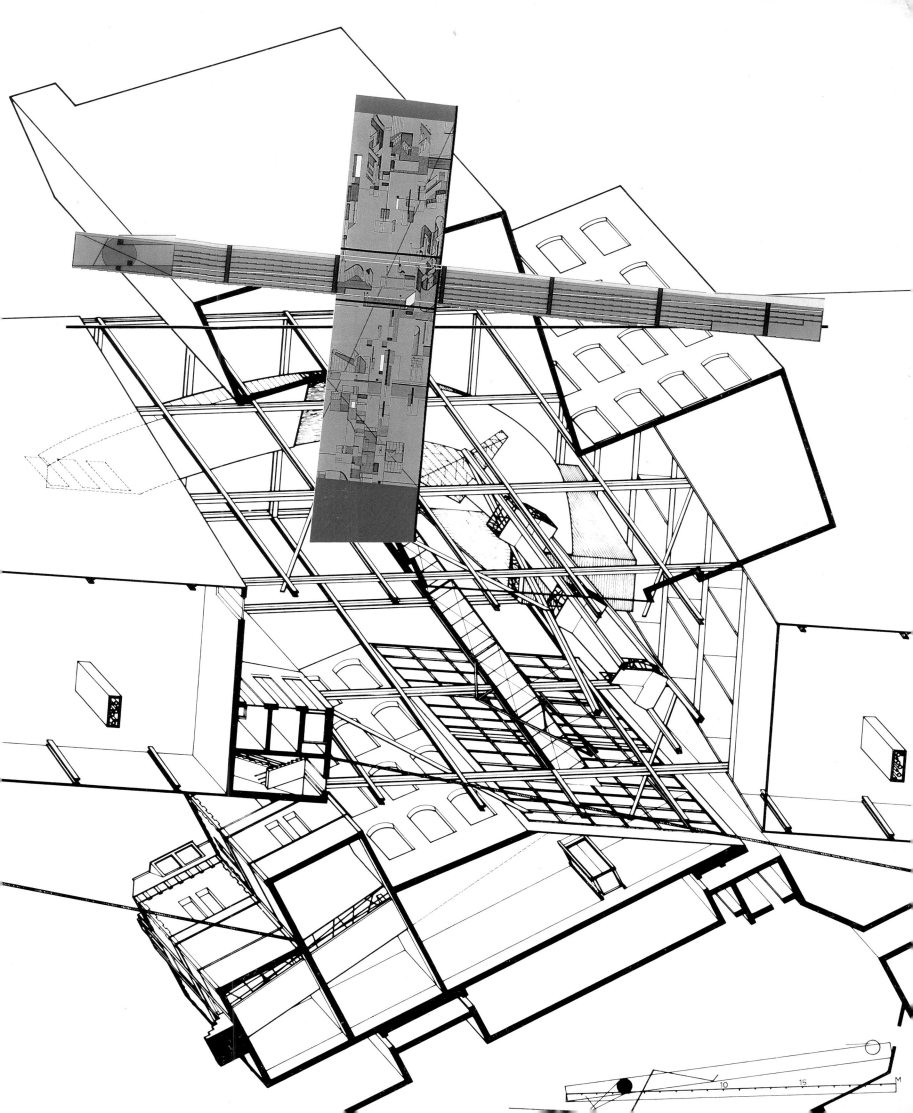

THE EXTENSION TO THE BERLIN MUSEUM WITH THE JEWISH MUSEUM, 1989

The official name of the project is the 'Extension of the Berlin Museum with the Jewish Museum Department', but I have called it 'Between the Lines'. I call it this because it is a project about two lines of thinking, organisation and relationship. One is a straight line, but broken into many fragments; the other is a tortuous line, but continuing infinitely. These two lines develop architecturally and programmatically through a limited but definite dialogue. They also fall apart, become disengaged, and are seen as separated. In this way, they expose a void that runs through this museum and through Architecture – a discontinuous void.

The site is the centre of the old city of Berlin on Lindenstrasse near the famous baroque intersection of Wilhelmstrasse, Friedrichstrasse and Lindenstrasse. At the same time, I felt that the *physical* trace of Berlin was not the only trace, but rather that there was an invisible matrix or anamnesis of connections in relationship. I found this connection between figures of Germans and Jews; between the particular history of Berlin, and between the Jewish history of Germany and of Berlin. I felt that certain people and particularly certain writers, scientists, composers, artists and poets formed the link between Jewish tradition and German culture. So I found this connection and plotted an irrational matrix which was in the form of a system of squared triangles which would yield some reference to the emblematics of a compressed and distorted star: the yellow star that was so frequently worn on this very site. I looked for addresses of where these people lived or where they worked – for example someone like Rachel Varnhagen I connected to Friedrich Schleiermacher, and Paul Celan to someone like Mies van der Rohe and so on. I was quite surprised that it was not too difficult to find and plot the addresses of those people, and that they formed a particular urban and cultural constellation of Universal History. So this is one aspect of the project.

Another aspect was Arnold Schönberg. I was always interested in the music of Schönberg and in particular his period in Berlin. His greatest work is an opera called *Moses and Aaron,* which he could not complete. For some reason the logic of the text, which was the relationship between Moses and Aaron, between, one can say, the revealed and unimaginable truth and the spoken and mass-produced people's truth led to an impasse in which the music, the text written by Schönberg could not be completed. In the end, Moses doesn't sing, he just speaks 'oh word, thou word' and one can understand it actually as a text as opposed to the norm of opera whose performance usually obliterates the text. When there is singing one cannot understand the words, but when there is no more singing, one can understand very well the missing word which is uttered by Moses, which is the call for the deed. So that was the second aspect.

I did a third thing. I was interested in the names of those people who were deported from Berlin during the fatal years, the Holocaust, that one knows only historically. I received from Bonn two very large volumes called 'Gedenkbuch' – they are incredibly impressive because all they contain are names, just names, dates of birth, dates of deportation and presumed places where these people were murdered. So I looked for the names of all the Berliners and where they died – in Riga, in Lodz, in all the concentration camps. So this was the third aspect.

The fourth aspect of the project is formed by Walter Benjamin's *One Way Street.* This aspect is incorporated into the continuous sequence of sixty sections along the zig-zag, each of which represents one of the 'Stations of the Star' described in the text of Walter Benjamin.

To summarise this four-fold structure: the first aspect is the invisible and irrationally connected star which shines with absent light of individual address. The second one is the cut of Act Two of *Moses and Aaron,* which has to do with the not-musical fulfilment of the word. The third aspect is that of the deported or missing Berliners, and the fourth aspect is Walter Benjamin's urban apocalypse along the One Way Street.

In specific terms it's a very large building, more than 10,000 square metres. It is budgeted for something like 120 million Deutschemarks. The building goes under the existing building, crisscrosses underground and materialises independently on the outside. The existing building is tied to the extension underground, preserving the contradictory autonomy of both the old building and the new building on the surface, while binding the two together in depth, underground. Out of the terminus of history, which is nothing other than the Holocaust with its concentrated space of annihilation and complete burn-out of meaningful redevelopment of the city, and of humanity – out of this event which shatters this place comes that which cannot really be given by architecture. The past fatality of the German Jewish cultural relation in Berlin is enacted now in the realm of the Invisible. (It is this remoteness which I have tried to bring to consciousness.)

The work is conceived as a museum for all Berliners, for all citizens. Not only those of the present, but those of the future and the past who should find their heritage and hope in this particular place, which is to transcend involvement and become participation. With its special emphasis on housing the Jewish Museum, it is an attempt to give a voice to a common fate – to the contradictions of the ordered and disordered, the chosen and not chosen, the vocal and silent.

So the new extension is conceived as an emblem, where the invisible, the void, makes itself apparent as such. The void and the invisible are the structural features that have been gathered in the space of Berlin and exposed in an architecture in which the unnamed remains in the names which keep still.

In terms of the city, the idea is to give a new value to the existing context, the historical context, by transforming the urban field into an open and what I could call a hope oriented matrix. The proposed expansion, therefore, is characterised by a series of real and implied transformations of the site. The compactness of traditional street patterns is gradually dissolved from its Baroque origins, and then related diagonally across to the housing development of the sixties and the new IBA projects.

In other words, to put it simply, the museum is a zig-zag with a structural rib, which is the void of the Jewish Museum running across it. And this void is something which every participant in the museum will experience as his or her absent presence.

This is basically a summary of how the building works. It's not a collage or a collision or a dialectic simply, but a new type of organisation which really is organised around a centre which is not, the void, around what is not visible. And what is not visible is the collection of this Jewish Museum, which is reducible to archival and archeological material since it's physicality has disappeared.

The problem of the Jewish Museum in Berlin is taken as the problem of culture itself – let's put it this way as the problem of an avant-garde humanity: an avant-garde that has been incinerated in its own history, in the Holocaust. In this sense, I believe this scheme joins architecture to questions that are now relevant to all humanity. What I have tried to say is that the Jewish history of Berlin is not separable from the history of Modernity, from the destiny of this incineration of history; they are bound together. But bound not through any obvious forms, but rather through a negativity; through an absence of meaning of history and an absence of artifacts. Absence, therefore, serves as a way of binding in depth, and in a totally different manner, the shared hopes of people. It is a conception which is absolutely opposed to reducing the museum or architecture to a detached memorial or to a memorable detachment. A conception, rather, which reintegrates Jewish/Berlin History through the unhealable wound of faith, which, in the words of Thomas Aquinas, is the 'substance of things hoped for; proof of things invisible.'

PIRIT. Spiri tspi rit spi rit spiritsp irits, Piritsp ir it spi Ritspi'r itsp-iritsp iritspi Iritspi rit spirit's pirit spiritsp. Iritspir itspir itspiri tspi Rits pi rit spirit spiritsp iritsp; Irits, pirit spiritspir, itspir itspi, Rit spirit spiritspir itspiri tspiri, Tspirits pir it Spiri't spirits. Pirits pir its pir itspi ri tspi, Ri tspi ritsp irit spirit spi ritspirit Spi ritsp ir itspir it sp iritspir; Its, pirits pir itspiri tsp irit spirit spiri tsp, Ir itspi rit spirits-pi ritspir itspi ritspir. Itsp iri tspi rits, pir itsp irit spirit Spi rits pirit sp iri tspir. Itsp iri tspir itspirits pirit spir Itsp iritsp iritspirit sp irits. Pi ritspiri tspi rits piri tspiri Ts piri tsp Iritspi ri tsp irit, Spi rits piritspiri tsp iritspirits Piri tspiri tsp iritspirit spiri Tsp irit spiri tsp iritsp iritsp, Iri tspiri tsp iritspir itspi rits'pi ritspirit. Spir itspiri tspi ritspi, ritspi rits pirit, Spir its piri tspiri't spiritspir itsp, rit spi rits piritspi ri tsp irits. Pir, its pir itspir its pirits pirits Pir itspir its pi ritsp iri tsp; Iri tsp iri tspir itspi rit spiri Tspi rit spiri tspir its pir, Itspi rits pir itspiri tspir, its pirits Pir itsp-irits pirit spir. Itsp iri tspirit spiritsp irits Piritsp iri tspir it spirit spir. PIRITS. Pir its pir itsp iri tspirit spi ritspi, Rits pirits pi rits, piri tspiri ts pirit, Spir itspi rits pirits p-iritsp. Iri tsp irit spir its piri tspi, Rit spiri tsp iritsp, irits

(Pirit spi Ritsp irits.)

PIRIT. Spiri tspi rit spi rit spiritsp irits,

Piritsp ir it spi Ritspi'r itsp-iritsp iritspi

Iritspi rit spirit's pirit spiritsp.

Iritspir itspir itspiri tspi

Rits pi rit spirit spiritsp iritsp;

Irits, pirit spiritspir, itspir itspi,

Rit spirit spiritspir itspiri tspiri,

Tspirits pir it Spiri't spirits.

Pi___ ___s pir itspi ri tspi,

___ ___irit

Its, pirit

Ir its___

Itsp iri tspi rits ,pir___

Spi rits pirit sp iri tspir.

Itsp iri tspir itspirits pirit spir

Itsp iritsp iritspirit sp irits.

Pi ritspiri tspi rits piri tspiri

Ts piri tsp Iritspi ri tsp irit,

Spi rits piritspiri tsp iritspirits

Piri tspiri tsp iritspirit spiri

Tsp irit spiri tsp iritsp iritsp,

Iri tspiri tsp iritspir itspi rits'pi ritspirit.

Spir itspiri tspi Ritspi, ritspi rits pirit,

Spir ita___ ___ ___

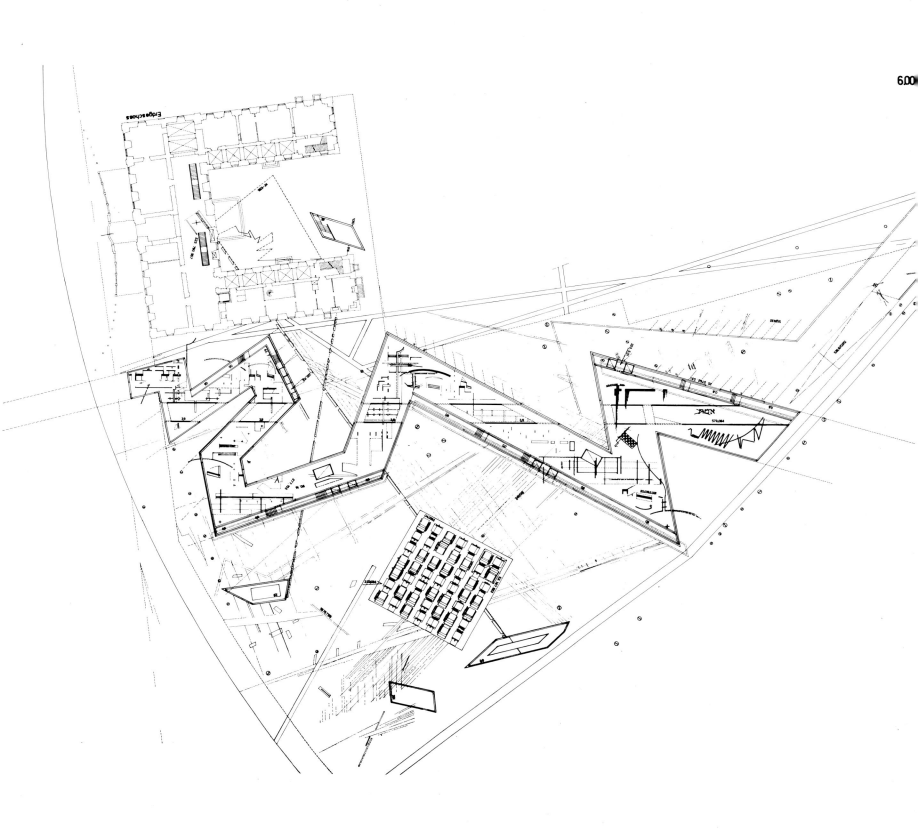

Erw illtopow erwilltop Ò werw illto: "*Powe rw illtopowe r wi*
"*opo w 'erw, ill topowerwill topow.*"

ERW.

ll topowe rwill top   opowerwill topo werw il lt o pow
will topowe rw il.   opower wil ltopow er w illt
owerwil.

Powe r willt o   top owerw il ltopowe
willtopo werwi   erwill topowerw ill to p
werwill topowerw   - po Werw ill to - po werw
lltopo werwil."

Powerwillt opo wer w   er will topow
rwil lto powe rwil lt   po wer will to
werwill top ower

Erwillt opowerw   erwi l   ow erwi l lto
we rwil l topo   lt opo wer   illt, opo werw
lto powe rwil ltop owe.

RWI.

lto po wer Willtopowe *rwllltop*,   topower, wil lt
owe: *rwillt opowerw illto powerwill*   il. Ltopower, *Wi*
LT.

OPO.

We rwillt opowe rwilltop ower willtopo werw il ltop, owe r w

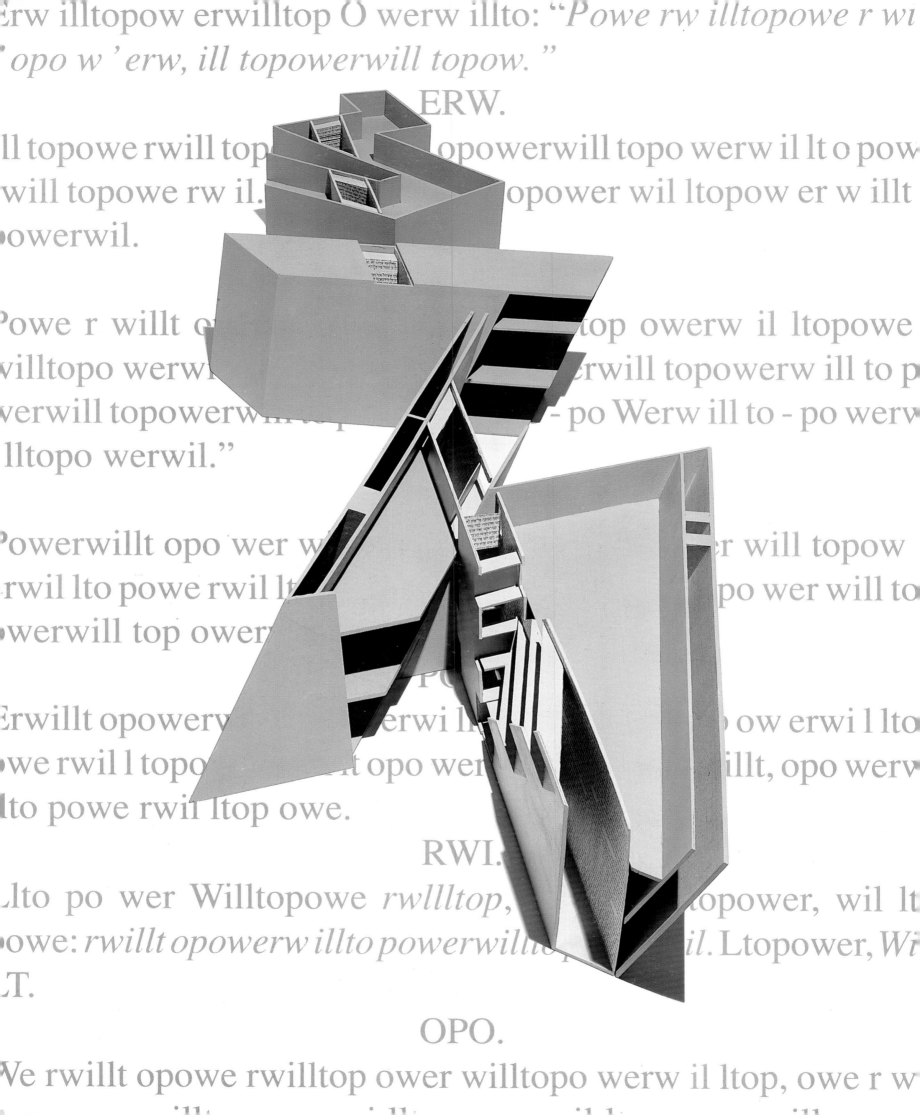

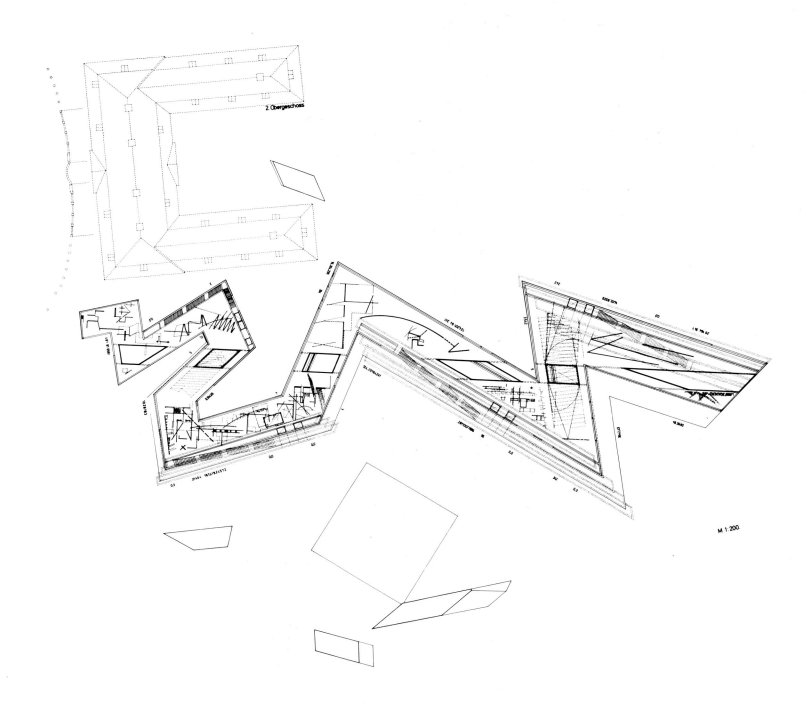

2. Obergeschoss

M 1:200.

topo werw il lt o powe rwill topowe rw il.
L topowerwillt opower wil ltopow er w illt
o powerwil.

Sedition is rooted in education which only appears to equal the whistle – sound dissolving the face's angry citadel.

A fully equipped talent is attuned to the sea. Rum for sketchy farewells, static abattoir. I am praising the city by spilling six phantoms on snows of evident docility.

– Taste excess with your cranium or advise the togaed attacker stranded on an oriental amphora that tall Saxons float in shame, ring shaped columns do not bend, Ghenghis Khan ridicules restrictions –

Are you entranced by fourteen hundred theorems, a dappled rabbit, cows bleating in the attic, ineffable apples? After all, the Universal Savant is airborne on the back of a billion Sibyls who shape cameos for a few cents while flying.

As for repair in the loving eruption, open scissors. I think of drinking diorite: testing a pedestrian conundrum with theatrical homicide.

Sobbing, a condemned woman resolves to put lipstick at the scaffold. Pod instinct throwing ogive vaults across debility; awesome dots, orthogonals of salty fluid.

Erstwhile theophany: discharge from a roving beast's eye, beauty criticising the colossus. Audacious faeries made of nuclear chromosomes form into threads, split lengthwise, associate with Don Juan's ovoid.

Enamoured with the medically depilated reflection races – are occidentals tired of animal mortar? Is a pneumatic NT built for sliding down Reason's annulated cadaver?

Distraught as medals thawed in Eve's tresses are the professors fussing in Erebus, humming.

– Kiss egg-like, crushing the sea.

– What extinct gizzard can hush these innuendoes, guests?

– Flame, the puritan's guile!

LTO.

Powe r willt op owerwilltopowe rwilltop
owerw il ltopowe r willtopo werwi llto pow

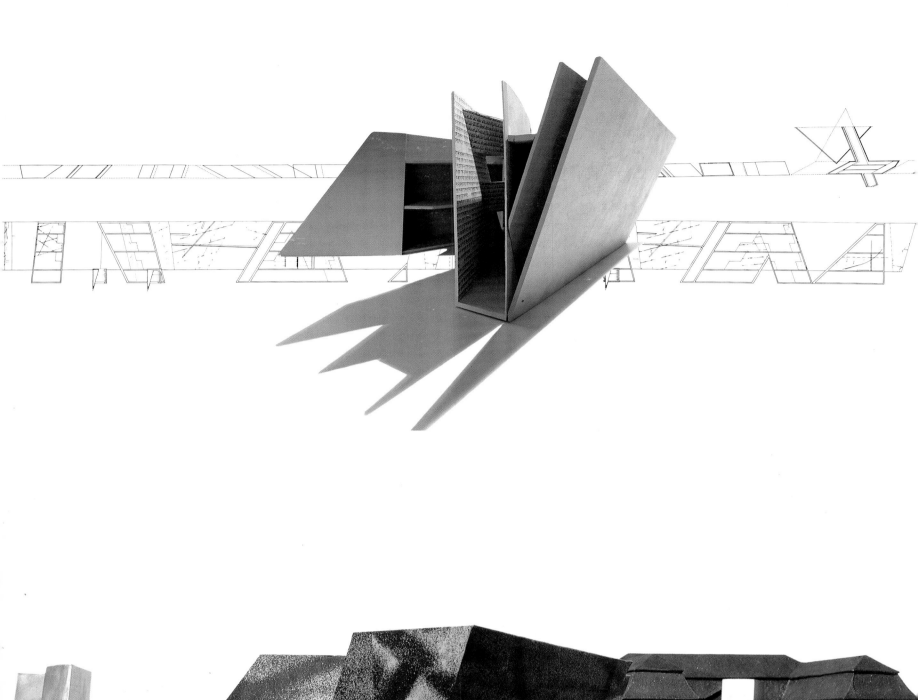

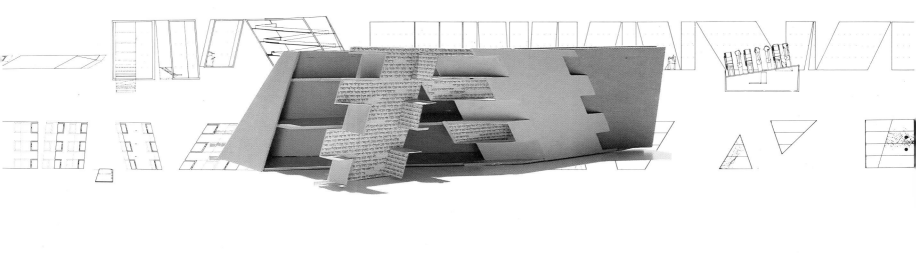

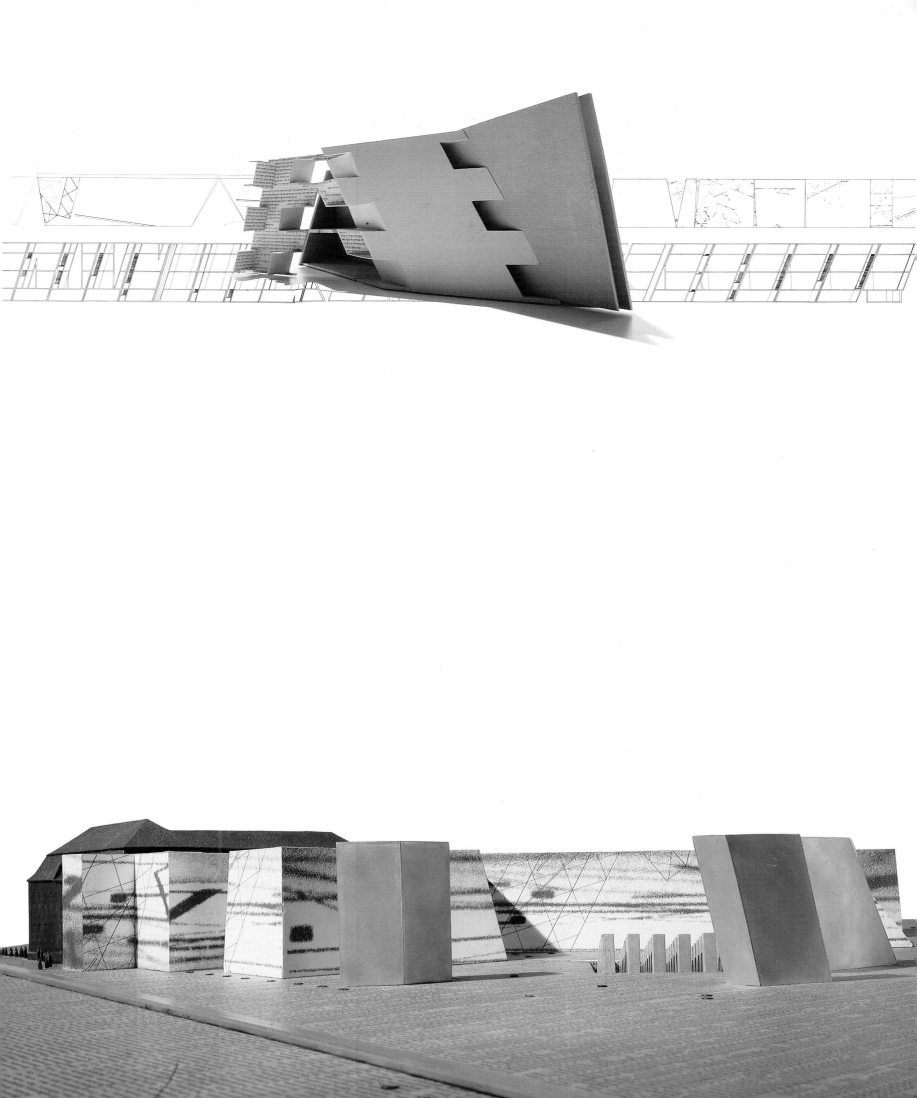

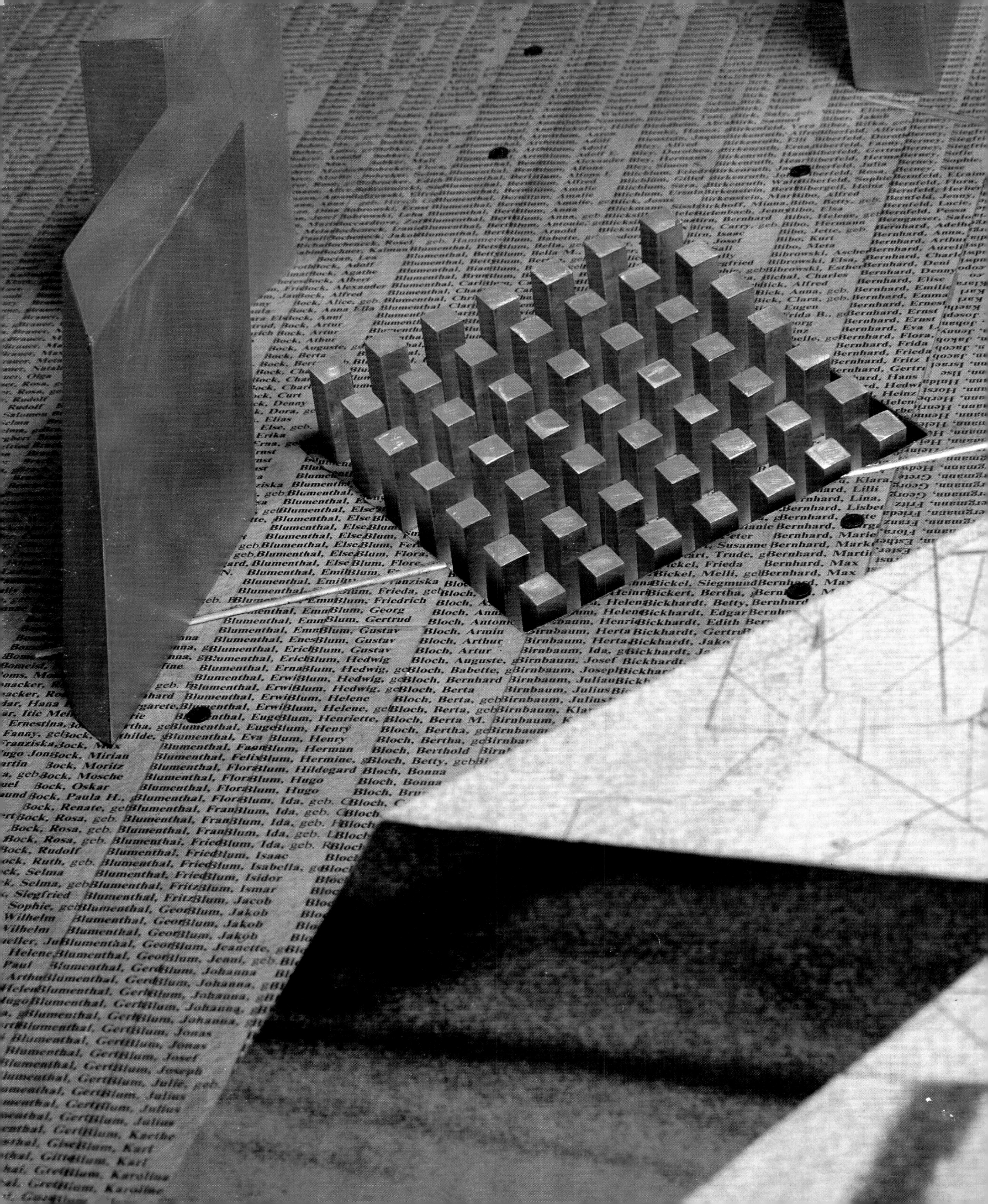

Lito po wer Willtopowe *rwilltop*, owe, rwilltopower, wil lto powe: *rwillt opowerw illto powerwillto powerwil*. Ltopower, *Wil. LT.*

The line of incision cutting the mind is straight and long – slice manipulating dearth. Strength, teaching, art, have no power to restore sight to the blind, eliminate lisp in the follower. Nothing is ever going to mollify the petty mole riding on your chin's weakness for space.

Saying 'amen' while repeating maxims on religion, Ahab is chopping his cerebrum into a pot in order to cook it. Boiled reason is excellent for a variety of diets. It is a dereliction – vegetarian blind to pity! – to refuse this morsel, cause of so many senseless, captivating disasters.

Space will not return in order to pick up castles stranded on the earth. It is generally projected by reason more feeble than gravity. Consequently, flying as experienced by man is no more than an exercise of the third leg dreaming of crawling inside any woman's rib cage.

Sometimes the Great Remote can be invoked through a knowledge of meanness and stupidity. Newlyweds delighting in violent matrimonial abandon can divorce after only two days without consulting their lion or seeking Vatican's permission. But don't worry mom . . . the taciturn old gentleman whose heady football I knew so well is no longer scared.

Frequent phenomena such as dieting peasants manning primeval Russian wheelbarrows which never touch the ground, Solomon destroying prose with ludicrous quoins, a man with several chins constitute the riddle which gushes out of the mouth, the point which never gets to it; if it did there would be no separation.

Seals do not heel. An electrical charge does not leap but personally formulates a detour round the play-square that has no right angles yet is drawn by a compass which crawls as well as the circle it draws.

OPO.

We rwillt opowe rwilltop ower willtopo werw il ltop, owe r wil lt opowerw illtopower wi llto powerwil lt opowe

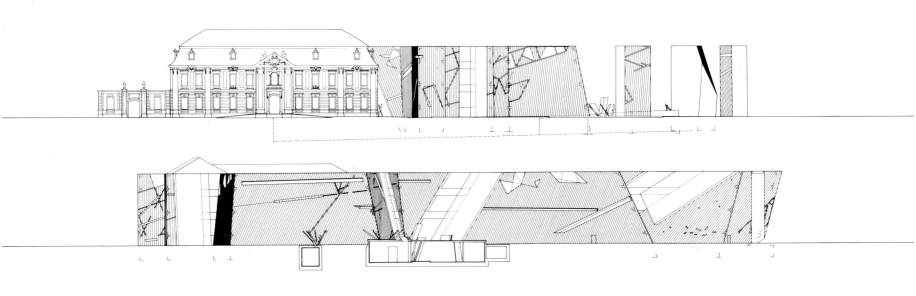

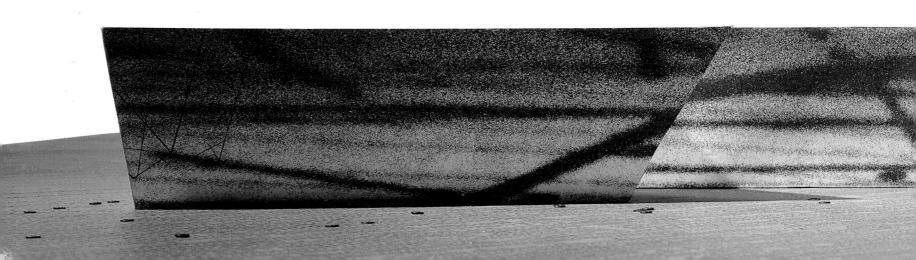

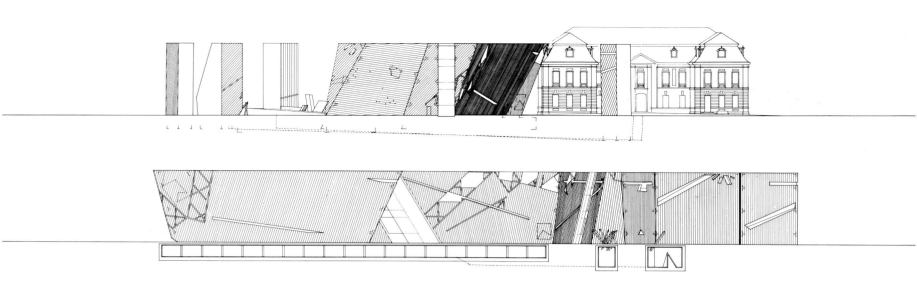

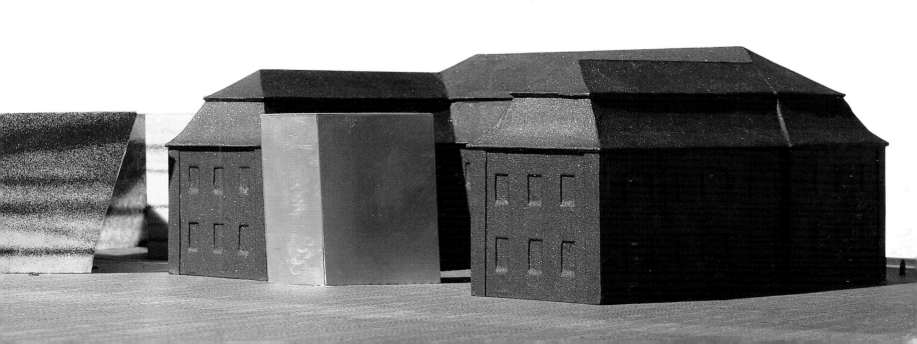

Bernhard, Fritz

Bernhard, Gertru... Bergmann, Ilse

Chaimb... Bergmann, Hugo Bergmann, Emmy

...nhard, Hans Bergmann, Elsa, geb

...ard, Hedwi... Bergmann, Horst

Berg... Heinz Helene

Helen... Bergmann, Isedor

Bergmann, Alfred

Bergmann, Edith, g

Bergmann, Regin Berger, Israel

Bergmann Berger, Israel

...ergman... Berger

Bergman... Berger

Bergma... Regin Berger

Bergmann, Klara

Bernhard, Lilli

Bernhard, Lina,

Bernhard, Lisbet

...Bernhard, Lotte

Peter Bernhard, Marie,

Susanne Bernhard, Mark...

...art, Trude, g Bernhard, Marti...

Bickel, Frieda Bernhard, Max

Bickel, Melli, geb Bernhard, Max

Bickel, Siegmund Bernhard, Max

Bickert, Bertha, Bernhard, Meta,

Bickhardt, Betty, Bernhard, Oscar

Bickhardt, Edgar Bernhard, Paul

Bickhardt, Edith Bernhard, Paula,

Bickhardt, Gertru Bernhard, Richar...

Bickhardt, Jakob Bernhard, Ruth

Bickhardt, Jakob Bernhard, Sara

Bickhardt, Kaeth Bernhard, Siegfr

Bickhardt, Thekla Bernhard, Siegfr

Bickhardt, Theres Bernhard, Susann

Bicz, Samuel Bernhard, Ursula

Biczunsky, Leopo Bernhard, Wilhel...

Biczunsky, Marga Bernhard, Willy

Bie-Milchner, An Bernhardt, Amal...

Bieber, Alfred Bernhardt, Anna,

Bieber, Alfred Bernhardt, Berta

Bieber, Annette D Bernhardt, Fanny

Bieber, Arthur Bernhardt, Guent...

Bieber, Brigitte, g Bernhardt, Hans

Bieber, Denny Bernhardt, Hans

Bieber, Erich Bernhardt, Hedw...

Bieber, Fanny Bernhardt, Herta

Bieber, Florentine Bernhardt, Hugo

Bloch, Lina, geb

...baum, Else

...baum, L...

Birnbaum, Herta

Birnbaum, Herta

Birnbaum, Ida,

Birnbaum, Herta

Birnbaum, Josef

Birnbaum, Joseph

Birnbaum, Juliau

Birnbaum, Julius

Birnbaum, Julius

Birnbaum, Klara,

Birnbaum, Kurt

Birnbaum, Lea, g

Birnbaum, Lina

Birnbaum, Marth...

Birnbaum, Marth...

Birnbaum, Maryl...

Birnbaum, Mathi...

Birnbaum, Max

Birnbaum, Meilic...

Birnbaum, Morit...

---

lum, Frieda, geb

lum, Friedrich

lum, Georg

lum, Gertrud

lum, Gustav

lum, Gustav

lum, Gustav

lum, Hedwig

lum, Hedwig, ge

lum, Hedwig, ge

lum, Hedwig, ge

lum, Helene

lum, Helene, ge

lum, Henriette,

lum, Henry

lum, Henry

lum, Herman

lum, Hermine, g

lum, Hildegard

lum, Hugo

lum, Hugo

lum, Ida, geb. C

lum, Ida, geb. C

Bloch, A...

Bloch, Anna

Bloch, Antonie

Bloch, Armin

Bloch, Arthur

Bloch, Artur

Bloch, Auguste, g

Bloch, Babette, g

Bloch, Bernhard

Bloch, Berta

Bloch, Berta, geb

Bloch, Berta, geb

Bloch, Berta M.

Bloch, Bertha, ge

Bloch, Bertha, ge

Bloch, Berthold

Bloch, Betty, geb

Bloch, Bonna

Bloch, Bonna, ge

Bloch, Bruno

Bloch, Camilla

Camilla, g

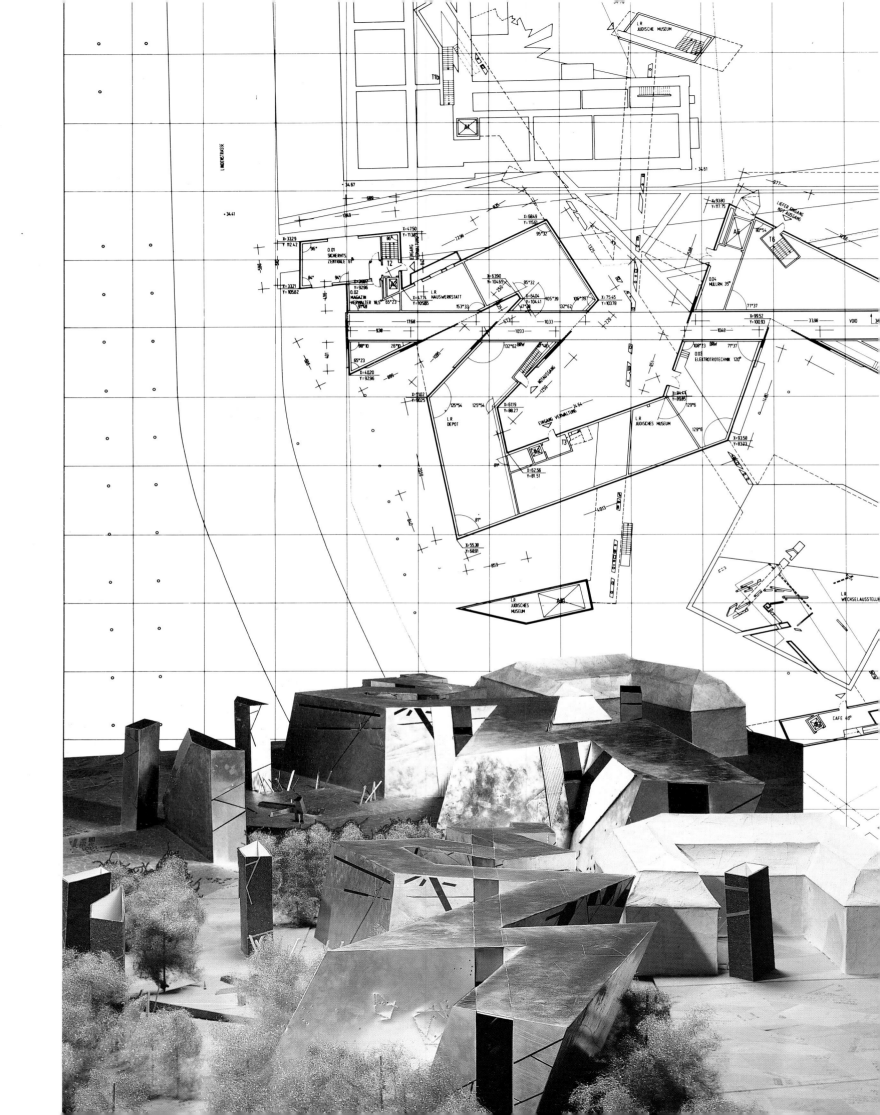

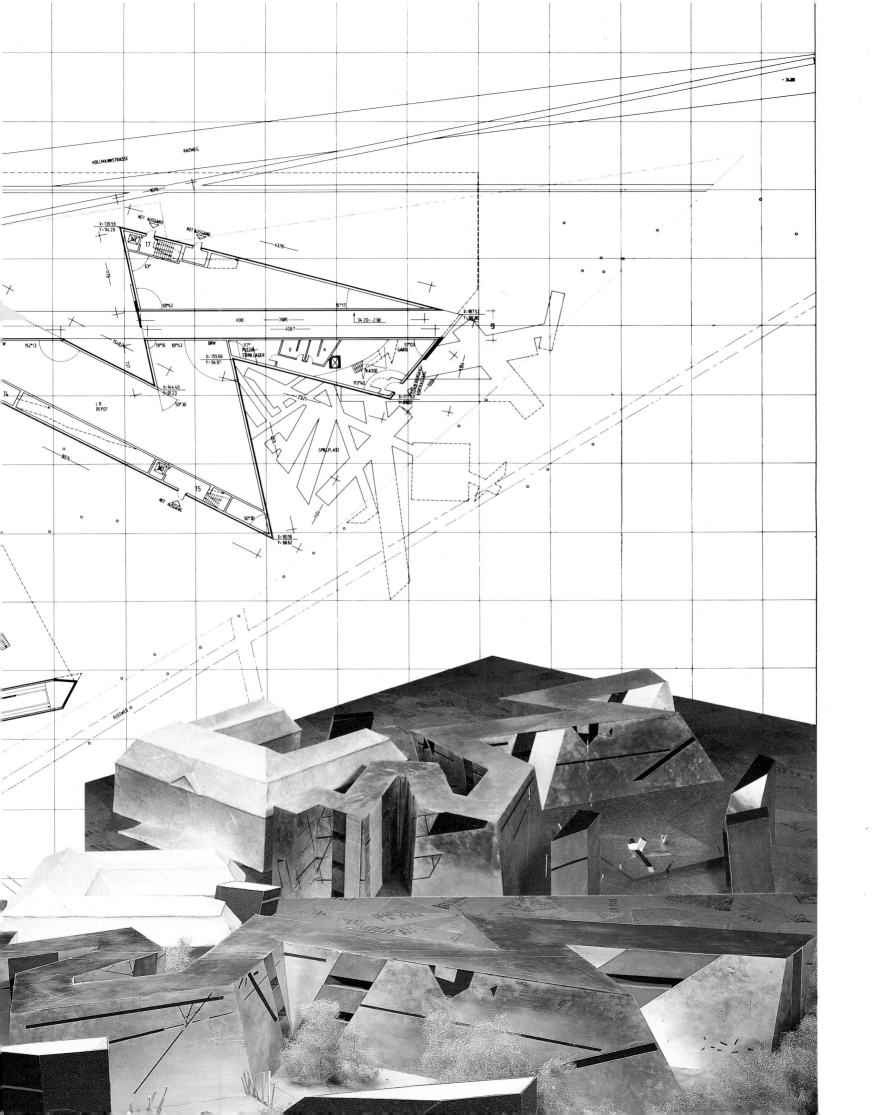

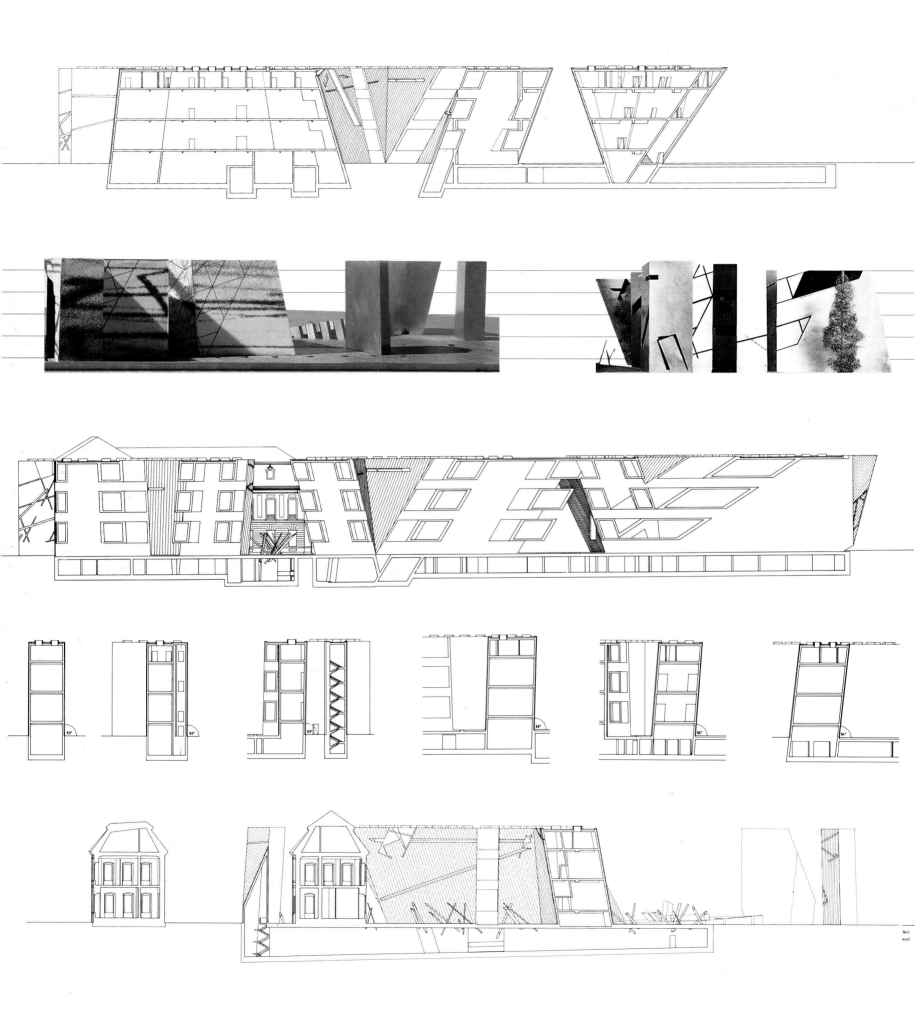

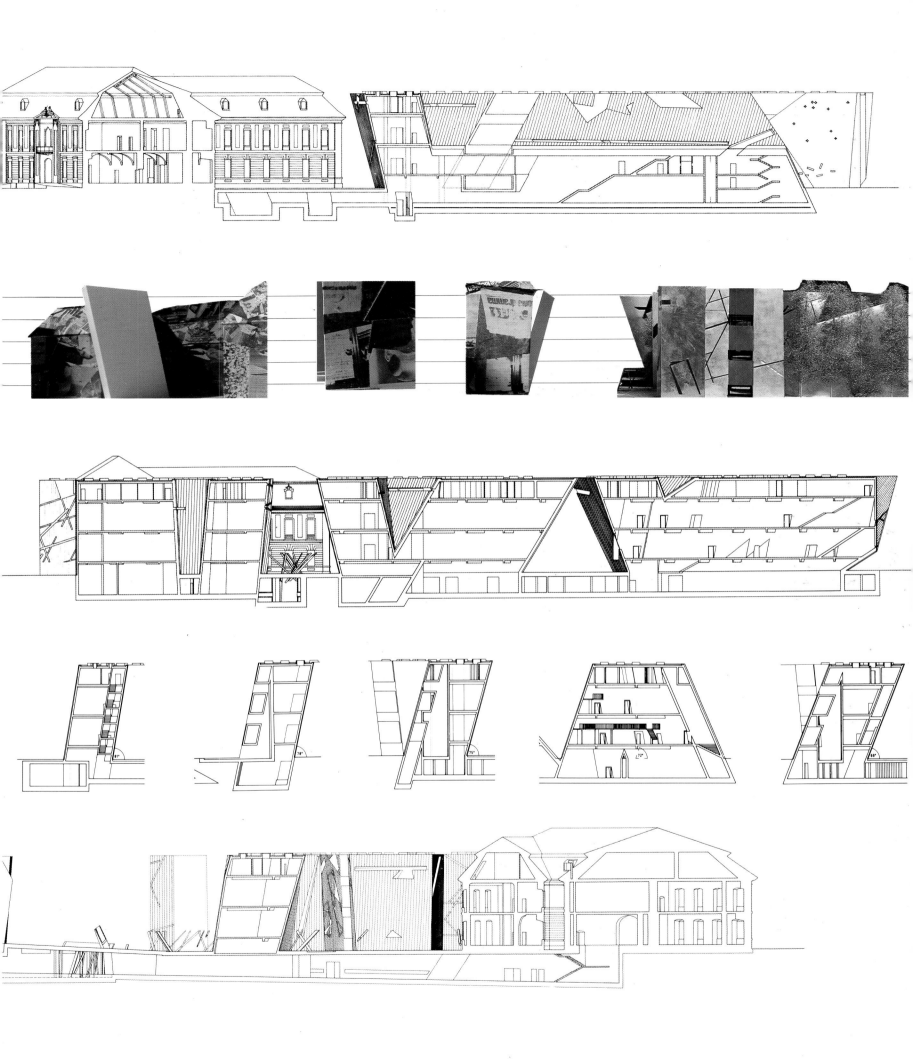

'What do you suppose that white line in the sky that you saw from the crack in the cattle car on your way to Stutthof really was?' the interviewer asked Elaine some thirty years later in her Brooklyn home.

'You see, in order to survive you must believe in something, you need a source of inspiration, of courage, something bigger than yourself, something to overcome reality. The line was my source of inspiration, my sign from heaven.

'Many years later, after liberation, when my children were growing up, I realised that the white line might have been fumes from a passing airplane's exhaust pipe, but does it really matter?'[1]

When the once potent truth of Architecture is reduced to a sign of its absence one experiences a parching, suffocating dryness: 'The psyche lusts to be wet . . . '[2]

When the depth of Symbol is drained from it, brought to the surface and flattened – the abyss into which it has fallen becomes visible: 'A gleam of light is the dry soul, wisest and best'.[3]

When Time itself is rendered meaningless by reversing its irreversible presence, then the practice of Architecture becomes the case of the false pleading the cause of reconciliation: 'Pythagoras was the prince of impostors'.[4]

As the Night is sinking on realities that have had their Day, one can still hear some lamenting a vanishing present. Others rejoice at the luminous perspectives – fascinating both as threat and charm – which emanate from the empty and endless. However, it is only when the processes that orient these transformations are themselves forgotten that consciousness is torn from its dogmatic slumbers by a return to the Unoriginal.

The contradictions inherent in everything which starts only from beings express the resolute procedure that remains necessary after the idols have fallen. What remains for those who no longer find greatness in Architecture is either to deny it or to create it – for using the ideal as a model is a symptom of a dishonest life. For those, like Nietzsche, for whom the Nihilism of Modernity is only a project to be overcome, a kind of unlikely spectre hovers – the Nemesis of the Vacant: for two thousand years humanity has been misled by a *phantom picture*. 'I call myself the last philosopher because I am the last man. Nobody talks to me but myself and my voice comes to me like that of a dying person.' (Nietzsche)

Architecture as a practice of control has projected over itself an immanent frame sufficient to reveal something without. What is at first an oppressive flash in this system yields in fact the things that belong together. Thus the truths that have been disclosed in space are the very ones that have been inscribed upon the flesh. This inscription, in the twentieth century, has been performed with all manner of precise instruments, including knives. It has been observed that one secretly reserves a tendency to disparage this dire state until one has undergone it. Architects too have suffered this ordeal by having followed Orders – the resulting disorder is yet to be appropriated even if it has been diagnosed and foreseen.

The recourse to surrogates is only a habit which can be given up. One can refuse to substitute, for the experience of Unoriginality, things that one has never experienced but which are known through originals. To substitute the 'essence' of Architecture for its actual non-existence would be futile and dishonest.

This work in search of Architecture has discovered no permanent structure, no constant form and no universal type. I have realised that the result of this journey in search of the 'essentials' undermines in the end the very promise of their existence. Architecture is neither on the inside nor the outside. It is not a given nor a physical fact. It has no History and it does not follow Fate. What emerges in differentiated experience is Architecture as an index of the relationship between what was and what will be. Architecture as non-existent reality is a symbol which, in the process of consciousness, leaves a trail of hieroglyphs in space and time that touch equivalent depths of Unoriginality.

Notes

1 Yaffa Eliach, *Hasidic Tales of the Holocaust*, Oxford University Press, New York, 1982.

2 Heraclitus, *Herakleitos and Diogenes*, translated from Greek by Guy Davenport, Gray Fox, California, 1979.

3 Heraclitus, from Charles Kahn, *The Art and Thought of Heraclitus*, Cambridge University Press, 1981.

4 *ibid*, note 3.

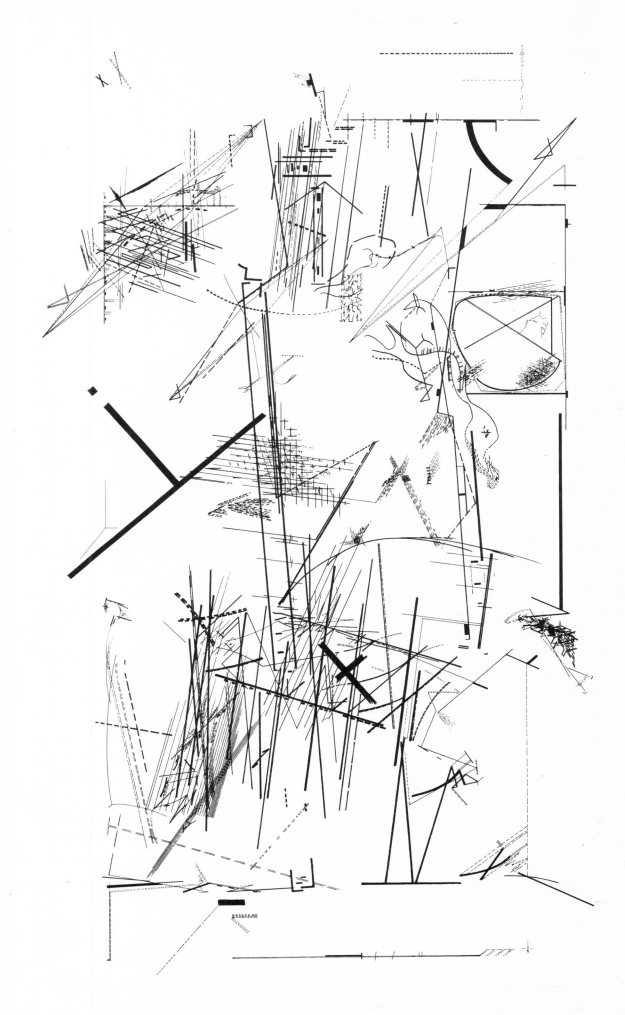

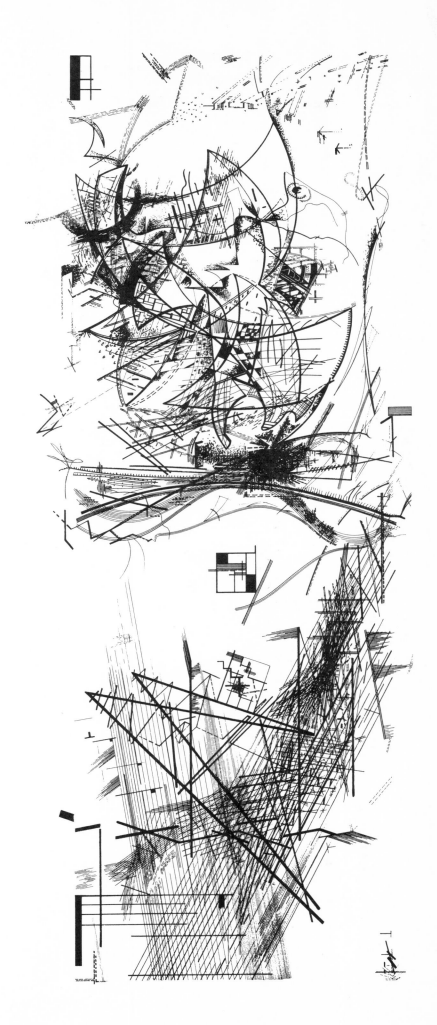

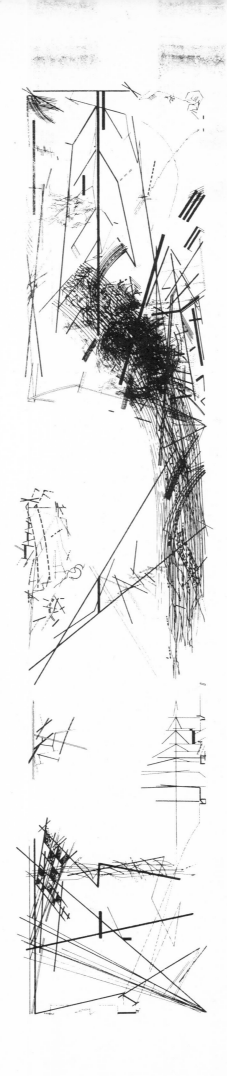

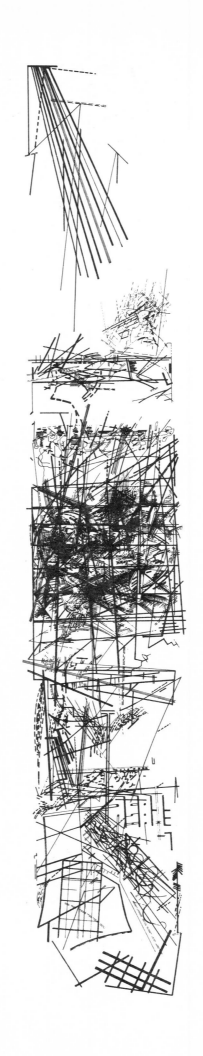

PETER EISENMAN
REPRESENTATION OF THE LIMIT: WRITING A 'NOT-ARCHITECTURE'

Throughout the history of architecture there has been a concern for the question of its limits, a concern that is manifest in any 'discipline'. Traditionally, in architecture, this has been studied from within the discourse itself – for this is the way in which the limits have been classically conceived. Consequently, any discussion of limits has always begun from the centre and worked outwards. For example, the drawings of Piranesi were understood in the eighteenth century to define a certain set of limits. They were seen to be not buildable (or not-building) precisely because a traditional convention of architectural representation, perspective, was intentionally contravened. Again, in the twentieth century the constructions of Lissitzky and Schwitters were limit provoking in that they transgressed, metaphorically, the laws of gravity – a convention of construction. Limits arrived at through transgression or contravention of convention are limits reached from within.

But it is possible that the discovery of the limits of a discipline can also be approached from without, that is by discovering what it is not. Rosalind Krauss, for example, in a recent essay attempts such a task for the new 'sculpture' by invoking two bracketing notions to landscape and architecture: not-landscape and not-architecture, which she uses to delimit a sculptural analytic matrix. Borrowing from her matrix, it might inform a search for the limits of architecture to deploy an architectural analytic matrix delimited by (sculpture: building: not-sculpture: not-building).

Alternatively, and more directly, it might be possible to locate limits of architecture by simply examining its complement, 'not-architecture'. Unlike a just not architecture, which is a state of having nothing to do with the subject, a 'not-architecture' would be intimate with architecture, would know it, would contain it, as architecture would know and contain a 'not-architecture'; it would constitute a relationship to being by not being. It is, of course, this intimacy, this 'insideness', that raises the possibility of limit discovery, although the model already suggests that a well-disciplined boundary is a delusory goal, that the limits will be found to be mutable, amorphic – an episode of transition in perpetual flux. It is within the domain of the transitory that the drawings of Daniel Libeskind must be situated. But further, and perhaps more interestingly, they must be *read*, and read as 'not-architecture'.

First, what is it to read a drawing? Traditionally, we read writing and see drawing. But if we transgress that custom, then we accrue to drawing the privilege of the autonomy of the reader. If we limited ourselves to seeing drawings as drawings then there would be no possibility of unhooking signs from objects (and thus 'not-architecture' from architecture), a privilege of reading. In architectural drawing, there is no metaphysics of 'hooking' – the image is not conceived of as 'hooked' to the object in the way that a sign is to a signified in writing. Traditionally, in a text, there is no necessary image relationship between the sign and its object or meaning; this is not the case in drawing since the image is a replication, representation or abstraction of an object – but it is not significant of it. The notion of 'unhooking' is crucial to discovering the 'not-architecture' in Libeskind's work, for it is in its free play of signing, its signing of signing, that we read these drawings as writings, and thus as a 'not-architecture'.

To insist that these are drawings, working documents for real physical form (whether as a three-dimensional model or a constructed building, ie, the traditional role of architectural drawing) would disappoint us. The three-dimensional artifact that would result could at best echo but could not contain, represent, or signify the content of these drawings, for the drawings exceed the existing cause and effect of drawing/building or drawing/model by a destruction of it. That exceeding sets them loose, unhooks them as an architectural writing from the traditional architectural drawing.

The prerogative of reading Libeskind's drawings as writing leads to the issue of the reader's privilege of naming. Why, for example, are these works architectural and not sculptural or simply concrete poetry. This is similar to the question: at what point is a shelter a 'house', or when is a structure 'architecture' and not merely building. Or in what context is a line drawn on the ground or lines on a piece of paper architectural rather than graphic or sculptural. Do they relate to architecture by a function: defining outside from inside, sacred from profane, shelter from not shelter? To invoke 'architectural' by a function is again to seek limits from inside, a return to form in a causal relationship to function. *Libeskind's drawings are intimate with architecture by the act, the will, and only the will of a reader to name them so.* Further, the act of reading these works, naming them writings, reinforces their status as architecture, for reading insists on their having a significance that as graphics they could not have. As graphics they could only represent architecture. The act of reading these drawings as writings, however, is insufficient to locate these particular works as 'not-architecture', a stronger condition than architectural, one beyond the naming authority of the reader. What is it about these works that is outside yet intimate? Why do we read Libeskind's works as 'not-architecture'?

To begin this 'not-architecture' reading, Libeskind's drawings must be situated within the present context of architectural drawing. Drawing in this sense is a narrative and often literal representation of a building or its parts. It achieves its status as architectural through the use of a conventional, well-defined vocabulary: windows, doors, walls, etc. But Libeskind's drawings are a critique of this tradition of drawing in architecture. Within the realm of orthodox architectural drawing perhaps only Aldo Rossi has achieved such a critique of drawing in architecture today – an inversion of the mode of representation wherein a realised building becomes a representation of a drawing. Libeskind, however, is not interested in inversions nor in mere representation. He is interested in de-assembly. De-assembly is for drawing what deconstruction is for writing; it is a knowing use, an emphasis of the fact that drawing is always in part writing.

Libeskind began the investigations that led to these works at Cooper Union where he initially developed a set of serial and gridded collages as fragments of both paintings and architecture, and of his own projects. This fragmentation was the beginning of an attempt to set elements free from their function in both their tectonic and formal sense – from the causality of function and form. In his next phase there were the Constructivist-like works, his first de-assemblies. Similar, superficially, to the investigations of the Constructivists, Suprematists, and Elementarists, the intent was different. While the former were interested in disassembly as a process of revealing the manifest essentiality of the isolated element, Libeskind's de-assembly demonstrated the inessentialness of transitory components; they were a denial of elementality. Next in the Micromegas works, any idea of causality of essentiality was superseded by raw process, a kind of 'writing'. These projects were studies in process-as-element, the essential of kinetic or dynamic, stop action flicker-films where there is no element or series of elements but only a directional serial energy. Finally, in these, his latest drawings, he further eliminates the essentiality of the vector in favour of an 'other' seriality. Their various positions defy constancy, either in element or in direction. They examine a contained transitoriness. The Micromegas were carefully projected within the bounds of zero and infinity. Now in these drawings even the non-limits of Libeskind's beginning and end have been erased, leaving only traces of the journey of his process.

These traces as writing are no longer within the canons of an architecture as defined by the classical tradition of drawings. As such these 'writings' or 'scores' require Foucault's new reader subject – an 'agnostic' aesthete, and a new object which is outside of the discipline of known origins and finite ends. This new object is no longer an object but a process – a trace of objects, outside the universe of tonal or a-tonal relationships. This new process/ trace cannot be understood within a traditional formal analysis of the drawings because these 'writings' do not believe in the compositional requirements for harmony; for hierarchy, ordination or closure. Nor is it fruitful to make an aesthetic judgement – that one looks better than another or that one seems right. These judgements assume an *a priori* notion of the value of images again according to a classical set of values of objects, that again, writing denies. Then what gives them any value at all? What distinguishes them from any set of lines?

It is precisely because they are not any random set of lines yet at the same time are not a precise set of lines conforming to a representation of an image. They are neither, they are other, and it is because of their otherness that they begin to define from outside the limits of architecture – that is they become a 'not-architecture' in the traditional sense of naming or writing. They are unhooked signifiers which begin to encircle their former signified. As such, they are an unsentimental trace of their own history. How far they can go before their progressive opacity (a quality of distance between signifier and signified) reveals its own transparency is the question of limit – their question of being.

KURT W FORSTER
CHAMBER WORKS FROM THE WORK CHAMBER OF DANIEL LIBESKIND

Die Zahlen, im Bund / mit der Bilder Verhängnis / und Gegenverhängnis.
Der darübergestülpte / Schädel, an dessen / schlafloser Schläfe ein / irrlichternder Hammer / all das im Welttakt / besingt.

Paul Celan, *Atemwende*, 1967

Architects' drawings are now the darlings of a new art public. The lost children of two separate arts, architects' drawings have been adopted mainly, it appears, by those who are committed to neither but are instead enamoured of decoration. As architectural drawings gradually became more technical – chiefly instrumental for actual construction – they lost an attractive quality that distinguished many of them in the past, that of exploration and fantasy. Daniel Libeskind's suite of twenty-eight drawings recovers the sphere of imaginative transcription and, in the process, opens up an unblinkered view of a realm in which signs compose a score of spatial music. As such, they have nothing to do with the current vogue that proffers technical kitsch and private reminiscences as instant art. Instead, *Chamber Works* composes a series of *inventions* which are at once fixed in their number and parts, yet open-ended and indefinite. Both the horizontal and the vertical series change from a full field to a narrow disappearing strip of markings. Beginning and end mark neither origin nor terminus but only moments in a larger series of transformations. Thus, the individual sheets are not locked into a single place within the suite but connected in varied ways to all others. This principle of variation pervades all aspects of the series, per-forming and trans-forming it. This implies a set of distinctive elements: lines, accents, figurations . . . The willed order of parts generates a logic of its own, but this order, of which *numbers* are the original and ultimate incarnation, spends itself while taking shape. The logic of these drawings rests no longer in itself, as an abstraction, but is entirely translated into lines, figures, signs, and their rapports. A spatial order develops from the mesh of signs within every drawing and throughout the series, as if a prism were slowly rotated in front of one's eyes. The drawings submit to a continuous *anamorphosis*, vanishing into unfathomable depth or advancing and flooding our field of vision. The actual size of the signs represents a relative scale of external distance as well as of internal depth.

What relates Libeskind's drawings most directly to musical composition is their axial structure: a double hinge connects horizontal and vertical, every element exists as melody and/or as chord. But this affinity to music does not remove the drawings from the realm of architecture at all; horizontal and vertical also constitute the framework of architecture and their rapport needs to be equally well 'composed'.

Since there is no fixed beginning or end to the suite of drawings, only differing perspectives on an infinite series of transformations, it revolves around internal symmetries rather than evolving along conventional lines: whether read forward or backward, in linear or rotational cross-correspondences, the drawings take their places in a planetarium of perpetually moving constellations. If the pictorial architecture of Juan Gris' paintings attempted to lock its internal ramifications within the static frame of single images, and if dodecaphonic, serial composition – as in the instance of Anton Webern's *Symphony op 21* (second movement) – closed the mechanism of composition within itself, the drawings of Libeskind may belong to a next stage in the development of compositional structure. This stage submits all previously fixed elements and their rapports to a yet higher principle of variability, as in Karlheinz

Stockhausen's *Zeitmasse* (Measures of Time) of 1956. Libeskind stakes out *Raummasse* (Measures of Space) and thereby scores architectural relationships. This new principle of variation, which makes every form a 'variant' of another, spins out the yarn of compositional thought into subtle filaments of the imagination.

The drawings of *Chamber Works* breach the conventional boundaries of architecture, not only in their cyclical variation of all elements but also by their presence within an unbounded field. Libeskind has not simply left building as the sole object of architectural imagination far behind, but he has also projected it beyond the familiar terrain of sites and images. His drawings possess a genuine kind of inexhaustibility – surely, they claim no essence, they tempt with no ready riches – because they suspend the contradiction between system and liberty. Their singular quality springs from the inventive store which lies inside systematic thinking itself, yielding, perhaps, only to the touch of numbers, numbers which encode an enigma of our own imagination. To conclude as I began, I translate Paul Celan's poem cited at the start.

Numbers, in cohoots / with the purposes / and cross-purposes / of fated images.

The skull pulled over it / on whose sleepless temples / a will-o'-the-wispish hammer / rings out to the beat / of the world.

PS: *Sind Libeskinds Zeichnungen der Einbildungskraft liebstes Kind?*

JOHN HEJDUK
THE ALBATROSS SCREECHED

Within their explosions, micro-megas announced a celebration of an architectural mystery, the cubic space of a private universe. The geometric fragments illuminated a moment in the concavity of Poseidon's soul. The shards pierced the very heart of architectural practice as it had been known till that second, calcifying the drops of blood until the red was extracted and silently fell as mist throughout the structure, settling into a disappearance. The science of pragmatic realism realised it had been challenged, its perimeter defences penetrated, and its world imploding. The micro-mega plates moved on, readjusting substructures. The architecture and the architects of spirit – suppression out of necessity tightened their diminishing circle, hoping their power of negation would last. Fools rush out where angels choose to tread.

When earth plates move so does the ground we walk upon. Micro-megas moved out from the adjusting crevices as the black starlings move out from a falling tree . . . horizontal . . . then abruptly upward. With a startling transformation, the beaks separating from the head becoming pure triangles and pyramids, the head separating from the body becoming pure circles and spheres, the body separating from the legs and claws becoming pure rectangles and volumes. Only the wings remain intact, but now invisible, their form distinguished and felt only by the differential pressure of the air movement.

The Albatross screeched in horror for its lost symbolism. Melville and Hawthorne met at the dividing line, neither had the heart to erase it, both suffered it, cursed its surface thinness, appalled by its extended depth.

Micro-mega was the European's belief in the expanding universe. Libeskind's new work is the American's knowledge that landscape permeates. The American observes the fact. The worm is pulled from the earth by the bird digging its claws into the sod, the same winged creature plucks the insect in its flight, suspending the wings to a still-stop.

This phenomenological work of Libeskind has turned the body inside out, but with a difference. Before there was the possibility of a transcendence, of the release of a soul that could be free in the unknown heavens. Now, the new drawings produce the antithesis. The body discarded – as the skin carried by man in Michelangelo's *Last Judgement*. But here we also have the soul being discarded, carried by a landscape of inexplicable meaning.

These drawings of cosmic-panoramic visions are drawings that have geometrised Freud's wildest rational thoughts. They abound in fallen angels, but angels that are no longer represented in human form; these angels are the fallen angels of the mind. There is a terror and a fierceness. The apocalyptic vision of Turner's seas and skies at least were comprehensible, there was *a* sea and *a* sky. The literal vision of Turner is frightening enough; throughout all drownings we can still see the body.

Libeskind silences all; we *see* the very soul.

ALDO ROSSI
SEMPLICEMENTE UN PERCORSO

For my project, of 1966, for a residential quarter for workers, I used a Cartesian grid to determine the layout of the houses, as if for the plan of a city. The grid was the Roman one, of an elementary geometry, thus representing a particular historical and intellectual order.

The design was already finished when I realised that there was a disturbing element to the order, involving a sense of something that had been lost, which made a truly rational design impossible. I looked then at the central axis: I broke it, it became like a fractured bone or some mental derangement. I wanted to represent thus all that cannot bear repetition within the realm of repetition or invention.

This preface to a discussion of Daniel Libeskind's work has multiple implications: not only is it revealing of my interest in his work, in which intellectual, mathematical and speculative elements are interwoven and combined in a kind of formal chaos; it hints also at a parallel to my own experience of what is called architecture – a kind of connection which to others might appear strange or mad but which is on the contrary one of the few connections which seems to me possible. Thus it is, with an almost selfish interest, to enlarge my own understanding, that I write these notes – something I would not, indeed could not, do for most of my contemporaries.

If we look at Daniel Libeskind's work and read his writings, we realise (notwithstanding any cursory impressions) that he has ignored the avant-garde and the Modern Movement, indeed everything that is the outcome of positivism. His quotation of Thomas Aquinas' definition of faith as 'the substance of things hoped for and the proof of things invisible'[1] is not simply a fine literary reference but something of profound seriousness: what we might call God, or knowledge, stands both at its centre and its periphery.

Thus Daniel Libeskind's drawings exist in a larger sphere: they reveal the possibility, in a certain sense 'technical', of describing this sphere which is based still on number, the perfect Pythagorean number of the area of the triangle, of astronomical triangulation. There is on the one hand an interpretation of Heraclitus' *Fragments*, on the other a search within craft itself for a perfection, a rigour which in turn provides the substance of that craft. Thus, if we look at Libeskind's drawings we can see that their beauty has a very special relationship to aesthetics, like the old Gothic masters who multiplied line and number to provide a system of ordering inexplicable other than in its own terms, for this order anticipated the cathedral and also, more specifically, the building of the cathedral. Like the finished building, it existed within a sphere encompassing the Divine.

On the other hand, Libeskind's striking obsession with graphics connects him to that tradition of drawing that extends from Guarini to Giacometti. The study of the human anatomy, the radiographical representation of the skeleton, pursued by artists and scientists in the determination of a fixed image, requires years of work: I refer here to those connections between form and structure, between a beauty that is often no more than apparent and those slight deformations, whether of a functional or pathological basis, which together make up the human body. This body too is contained within that sphere which we can do no more than explore.

If in his drawings and writing Daniel Libeskind rejects that 'modernity' (in the negative sense) to which I referred earlier, he refutes at the same time any psychological or literary concerns within art or its critique.

Art and criticism based on psychology, characteristic of the whole of Freudian and post-Freudian literature, constitutes a last hope for the survival of modernism: if the search for meaning no longer exists, if technique, art and craft no longer exist, we must needs search for some private motivation for a work. It intrigues me to imagine how critics, face to face with Libeskind's drawings, might or will find some basis for a literary interpretation. What we have now in the field of art criticism is an impoverished literary tradition, seeking out the unusual, the bizarre, and the personal mingled with an avant-garde schema somewhere between the modern and the post-modern. But the questions posited by Daniel Libeskind override all this; he has questioned, *à propos* one of my works and its relationship to this basic problem, '. . . whether the "no longer" of modern architecture actually belongs to its very own "not yet"'.[2]

Thus, to return to my earlier parallel, when Libeskind saw in my *Teatro del Mondo* 'the pinnacle, its rigid flag a messenger of some deflated and long-forgotten Boreus',[3] I thought that a north wind of disaster, belonging to some geographical fantasy, must needs run through art and technique like the real or supposed crack running through that Roman grid. The analogy can thus be transformed into a vision of things which we can no longer remember because of some lapse of memory, but which could not, nonetheless, have been invented. The relationship between technique and invention is peculiar: it both hinders the inexperienced and controls the expert. Anyone seeking clarity must necessarily use superimposition, and superimposition clouds reality. Juan de la Cruz, who must be one of Daniel Libeskind's favourite authors, speaks of this action within a dimmed reality 'y la mas fuerte conquista/ en escuro se hacia'.

Observation, repetition, the desire for clarity: a flight from things in penetrating to their depths. But this dangerous pursuit, like silence, is part of that quest which modern man, in the Galilean sense, must attempt.

When Daniel Libeskind first showed me his drawings, I saw them in my mind overlaid on his expositions of the architecture and sculptures of the school at Cranbrook: often as we walked he would explain these works again and again, with such clarity of detail and such objectivity of impression that, in their overlays, both formed and reconstituted the singular landscape of Cranbrook. Perhaps it was in our common comprehension, or perhaps in our common understanding in work, that we both saw and came to know quite precisely the colour and form of a 'key' or 'cypher': and we are not afraid to look at it, to repeat it, immersed as it is in a complex of hieroglyphics. Yet in continually returning to it, we know we will lose it and we must ask if ours is a flight or a search.

Though when I look at certain things, including the drawings of Daniel Libeskind, I think that there is not so much a road towards the goal, crossed by many diversions but simply a path. The whole of this path will still be made up of technique, or art, or architecture, or some other thing which we might call our craft.

Notes

1 Daniel Libeskind, '"*Deus ex Machina*"/"*Machina ex Deo*", Aldo Rossi's Theatre of the World', *Oppositions* 21, 1980. 2 *ibid*. 3 *ibid*.

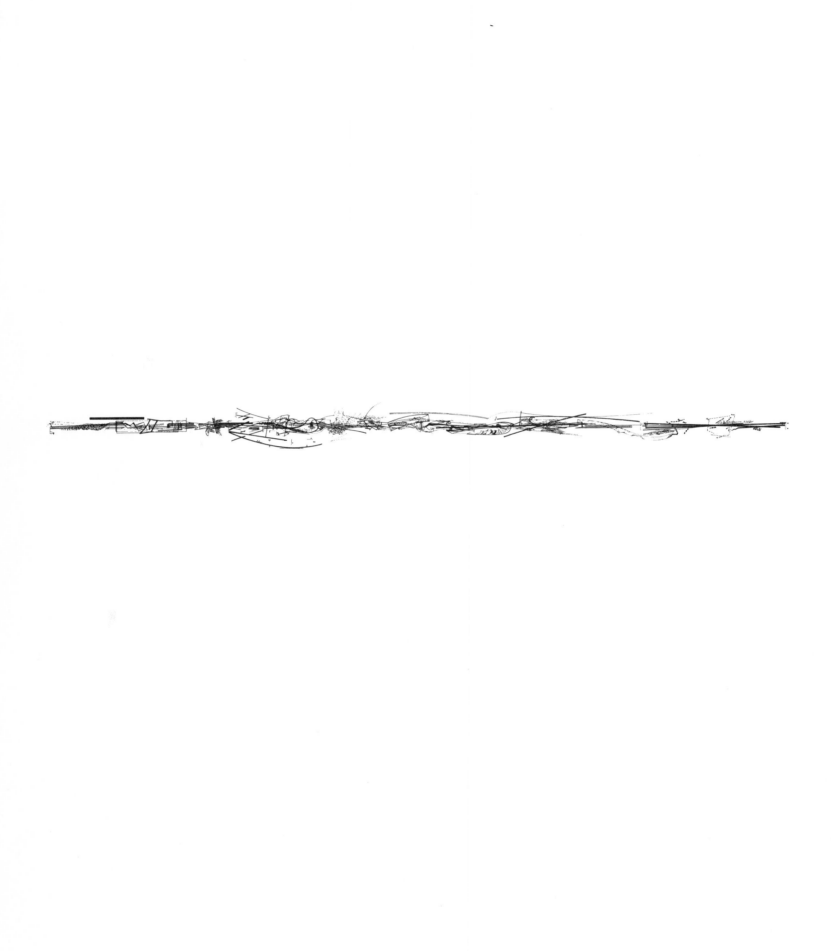

Berlin today: Peking yesterday: Leningrad tomorrow . . .

No sooner has one begun a work – touched pen to paper – than the effort lapses, inseminates itself, cancels and overcomes origins. Endings are interminably longer than their own history. Incorporating the undecidable in a uniquely proliferating system of displacements, architecture's groundlessness finally *becomes;* becomes a state one no longer hopes to be rid of. Abyss has still more weight: an obelisk cannot stifle the spreading desert. A mechanism finally reaches what 'no eye 'ere grieved for'. Distress has an effect which is virtuous and subversive at once.

Until today, Architecture was on the wrong track. 'Rising up to heaven or grovelling on the ground, it has misunderstood the principles of its existence and has been, not without reason, constantly derided by upright folk. It has not been modest . . . the finest quality that ought to exist within an imperfect being.'* Since its very appearance Architecture sought to construct mechanically the brain of stupefied dwelling. But it was not sufficient to mimic language (history and meaning) in order to create a place which is *not* wherever the calculating, mocking smile of the constructor *is.*

Architectural thought no longer exists – no longer exists as a self-deferential discourse, no more than does any other autobiography. Permanently infecting the maternal sources which render identity, technique itself contaminates the sense of dwelling across language, introduces mechanisms of transference between architecture and subject, reprieves fatherhood in the sense of conscious begetting . . . Rendering architectural mother-tongue by violating its limit, haunting the traceable which had its beginning in a dawning of guilt, architecture becomes past in the sense that today it has entered its coda. A code EX, a coded that cannot be decoded; an X, a CODEX which invalidates its origin/ality raises the un/original, founded as it is upon incertitude, upon the void, upon the language of the dead which yet refuses to be a monument to a dead language. There will be no more specialists in provoking grandeur through power, no fictitious images which would have been better to soothe their author's brain, no beams raised high above mortal existence. Eyes will revert to themselves on completion of the investigation and will perceive the grace of someone struggling to steady himself, herself.

The skeleton hanging: the carcass. The uncertainty of muscular movements in wounds or in the soft parts of the lower cerebral regions. Ultraviolent cities. Here X: *con architettura* . . . Lobsters in the Russian Stables. *Ex-con:* architecture. Camels under the ecumenical banner of the perpetually trapped, perpetually reset by the trapped rat, analogical *polis.* By disarticulating boundaries architecture's beauty comes to be identified with its congenital malformation. The result of aesthetic principles which have varied and will vary again, but not in accordance with the progress of mankind. Is the process annulling the traces of intellectual disturbances which hark back to the spherical and convex surface area which resembles an orange only in shape?

Nothing remains except deference: the deference of the immortals to the immortelles. Documents only map the neurotic ground which under the insignia of reason-foundation-nation usurps the ever unreadable yet ever re-consecrated text. Every community is questionable, and questionable precisely in its deadening, politically pre-arranged disappointments. The architect's refusal to indulge in the paradise of recirculated enchantment – in myth-paranoia – leads to a not-etymological, a-historical, foundation-less architecture; one moreover produced in a time of renewed anti-international and national crises. . .

The old architecture gently raised a child's face from the open coffin in the ground to sling hissing space . . . Here, the hasty burial . . . a conceptless vacancy left in its species by obsolescence. 'Is this how the flesh, my dear Socrates, partakes of the mass product eternal?' For there *is* no way. So it is that what is rendered compellingly, created as an incomprehensible polyhedron of intention, constantly ebbs away. Forget because. No knowledge allows two pillars to disappear like two pins, or two towers or two baobab trees while extending into practice that arabesque whose 'conclusion' is only a form of parody or pastiche. Carefully gnawing the skull of the viewer a critique is resumed and consummated in the form of n(X). A preview of the exhausted play of references dissolving the boundary between aesthetic idleness and the insomnia of consumption. A network of vexations unfolds: Production . . . is it not idleness? Inertia . . . is it not the dynamic? An unravelling of architecture takes place in the midst of its irreparable achievements which disclose a moral web. A vanishing divinity which in this tale within tale is caught up in an endless analogy of reproduction, subverted by an excessively swift proliferation of disappointments. How poignantly does this 'post-fall paradise peace' explode one's tenancy in the possible! No rage for the ideal in this complex which only idealises the attempt to rid itself of the idea: a catastrophy in the guise of a continuity mechanism. Is the work of architecture a regretful longing for the beautiful? For architecture itself? Beautiful like . . . (tentacular filaments, the centipede's countless feet, dutiful servants). The social apparatus declines architecture in its singular, continuous, present-less tense; drawing with its precision instruments directly on the body, or rather on the soul, which merges into a linear unity with the theorems of mechanics.

A longing for architecture . . . yet a conception and generation that architecture never achieves. By extending, differentiating into distinct layers, moving from light to light, remounting in progressive shades, a perpetual dissection takes place. Technique is passing successively, in minute increments, through a countless number of oblique planes. The superstition of health, the mark which reveals no history, the imploding representation project unto the void: a halfway space. Between work: between *is: inter-est*. Envoys that fly through the desolation of architecture? A process willed but not known in its being. A machination which orders the compulsion yet holds away by completing the circle and the square: the circle without radii, the square without diagonals. Single element – a wheel which is square – propelling everything . . . daring feat of aeronautics . . . Here also a line of flight which metaphysical thinking hangs on to as it splinters identity – appropriating the inflexible laws of optics by probing the impenetrable darkness associated with the echoes of the street. *Here goes Sum* (here go some): in pain, under the dominance of hesitancy, bereft of an escort. But move the hand clinically, survey surgically the two estates separated primordially and align them now in a chaosmic vision: the inexorable moment of *déjà vu*. Look at the eye! 'A distressed ship firing off her alarm gun, but sinking slowly: glued to the grating still more eagerly, wondering who its master might be; horse galloping along the shore as it is fleeing the human look.'*

Revenge with respect to the gods of thresholds.

Economy which draws out what eludes determination, is undecidable, yet still homogeneous with the world of limits. Are these prophecies, priestly accounts, divinatory scripts, automatically reconstituted myths (according to the laws of amputation)? Initiate architecture to love. Proclaim against medical terminology, clichés of condolence, the style of children's handwriting, the jargon of sports journalism. Ceremonies of farewell to a royal visitor ridicule the model imitated: the greatness of copies is that they point to the absurdity of originals. A panorama in the vein of an epic vignette. Report of a cataclysm. Architecture moves across the cut-off and the cut-up, mediating a realm formerly inhabited by sons of craft heavy with stupor. No mechanical art can here substitute for Need begging at the door, which the continual appropriation and interrogation of the mundane misappropriates. A wearywide surface opens – one whose shifting superpositions become a paradigmatic field of displacements. The retracted layers of Architecture multiply and divide, creating a fissure in the seemingly non-malignant network of ideacontinuitycontext. This faultline permits the outrageous emergence of meaning by disappearing beneath the weight of ambivalent codes playing on its surface. The calculated, the built, the thought, the said, become gaps indebted to what cannot be communicated, are thus condemned to replay it till the end. Plagiarism, forgery, terrorism of confession follow – as does the anonymous interlocutor with his relentless 'traces', revealing the sway of the past over the present, of madness over analogy. The recognition of Need as the necessity that Resource follows in that bed of Dwelling is only inserted as a derisive history, one prone moreover to citations of lyricism in its fall through space. Architecture seems to exist only through a piece of forgetful negligence on God's part: for if God had foreseen planning he would not have created the burning bush or the promised land.

Continually disposing what can be posed in its own 'discourse of forms', today's architecture escapes the claws of integration, disorients Galileo through inexplicable intensification of centrifugal force, grows by the cube of the distance from the centre, trans-locates its organs, coils-up place. (Only a special kind of virtuosity does not let the sun set behind the horizon.) Architecture enters space in which everything is transmuted by being projected directly unto the plane of the destructible, displacing one's hold over being-here. Ground splinters, epiphany becomes proof of repetition, vision a game.

Is architecture a lunatic playing with sheets of glass? A dissemination of architecture progressively extends its hallucinatory operations. But the translation of this process into a system can find no equivalence between experience and the trauma of repression. Abrogate the tacit agreement that hinges upon the compromise of signs! Devastating: Visceral. Return the repressed. Now architects resemble dust particles in a closed box made visible by a ray of light while Architecture appears as a venerable beam set at the highest roof – standing on end – soon to resume its horizontal position (so dear to the startled spiders). Only anticipation mobilises the equivocal poetry of building and in the process raises the 'Babel' motif. Beyond the immense and daring challenge of contemporary work one can sense the proliferating ascendancy of detachment. Is it possible that now *no one's 'turn' is dwelling?* More. What is built is itself an instrument of re-volt. A 'turn' which cannot be entered. For who can really say again 'I have seen the hangings draped in the shape of a crescent moon but without their definitive symmetry in the quaternary?'*

The ambiguous, promiscuous, violent relation one has with architecture works a tortured admission: the seal releases by sealing: the sign effaces by de-signing. The signature of architecture expropriates – can no longer be thought of as being in terms of presence. Architecture as no longer/as no/longer not. Beautiful Architecture Without Beauty.

Note

* Comte de Lautréamont, *Les Chants de Maldoror*, translated by Alexis Lykiard, Apollo Edition

```
B.E.I.N.                                                        BEINGBE, BEI NG BEIN
BEi   NGb  EinGbeing BEIN GBe  INg   BEi-  n GB  Ei      Ngbel      GB   EIn    GBe    ...  INg    BEi
Ngbel      NG    BEi   NG  BEi+ n GBe      INg  Beingb   El    NGb  EIn  GBe+i Ng  Be    Ingbei   NG
BEi   Ng   Be-   i NGbEi    Ngbein   GBEI NGb  Ein  GBe+i Eln GBe   Ingbei    NG   BE   INg  BE+  i
NG    BEi Ngbel  NGB  EIn   GBe INg-  b Eln GBe  Ingbei    NG   BEi   NG   BE-  i Ng  Be   Ingbei NGBE
InGb-e  NgBe    IngbEi     NGB  Eln   GBe  IN-   g BE  INg   BeingB    EIN  GBe  INg BEi+   n GB E   I   n
Gbeing     BEIN  GBe  INg   BEi+ n GBe       In    Gbeing    BE   Ing   BEi   NGb+e In  GbEinGb EIN    Gb
EiNg ... BEi      Ng   BeiNg    B    Eln   GBe   INg-  b Ei Ng    BeinGb     El   NgBe In  ... GBe   INg
BeIng      BEI   NGb   El   NGb+  e
B.E.I.N.                                                         BEINGBE, BEI  NG  BEIN
BEi   NGb  EinGbeing BEIN GBe  INg   BEi-  n GB  Ei       Ngbel      GB   Eln    GBe    ...  INg    BEi
Ngbel      NG    BEi   NG  BEi+ n GBe      INg  Beingb   El    NGb  Eln  GBe+i Ng  Be    Ingbei   NG
BEi   Ng   Be-   i NGbEi    Ngbein   GBEI NGb  Ein   GBe+i Eln GBe   Ingbei    NG   BE   INg  BE+  NG
BEi Ngbel  NGB  Eln   GBe INg-  b Eln GBe  Ingbei    NG   BEi   NG   BE-  i Ng  Be   Ingbei    NGB    E
InGb-e  NgBe    IngbEi     NGB  Eln   GBe  IN-   g BE  INg   BeingB    EIN  GBe  INg  BEi+ n GB E   I   n
Gbeing     BEIN  GBe  INg   BEi+ n GBe       In    Gbeing    BE   Ing   BEi   NGb+e In  Gb    EinGb EIN Gb
EiNg ... BEi      Ng   BeiNg    B    Eln   GBe   INg-  b Ei Ng    BeinGb     El   Ng   Be  In  ... GBe
INg    BeIng    BEI  NGb   El   N
B.E.I.N.                                                         BEINGBE, BEI  NG  BEIN
BEi   NGb  EinGbeing BEIN GBe  INg   BEi-  n GB  Ei       Ngbel      GB   Eln    GBe    ...  INg    BEi
Ngbel      NG    BEi   NG  BEi+ n GBe      INg  Beingb   El    NGb  Eln  GBe+i Ng  Be    Ingbei    NG
```

Eve, holly, ivy, apple. There will be no more cities on the surface only what is unfinished: ugly men, tours of Ellis Island, the Other. Even one's own mother tends to become cruel when one has interest in childhood, particularly early puberty. Meanwhile Reality is played by Major Leaguers using zero as a wall and nothing for a bat – while pretending that the Manager napping in the bleachers is the ball. The baseball game of dimensions, prophetically shielded by trouble-free membranes made out of poetic opacity, converts ambiguous identity into unequivocal yes-content. Yet if you depend on the internal reserves lodged inside the dim shrine some will call you a pig deposited in precise manner by representation; others will accuse you of being demented because you trust every indication – internal or not – which dangles like a *persona non grata* from the Tree of Life. Gloss over the geometry of silence thrown under every *foglio di carta*!

The line is always perpendicular to a vibration emitted by Dio who first kissed triangles, then became equilateral, circular, finally a repository of tradition in liquid. Drunk Castillians still consider the Vertical a form panacea because it provides God with an old-folks' home, ie, a mild *cannot*. This little hypothesis confirms that revelations always belong to some Ann, Cathy or Eve.

If you see the crossed out I as letter K or consider dollars a fearful code (curve and two parallel lines) you are likely to uproot infinity overtaking in the NO PASSING lane. I said before that the Real is a pigeon but what I meant is that its physiognomy nestles softly and flexibly along the region where verbs can dissemble their filial position. Nails, for one, are part of the frame yet also appear in it, especially when a T shakes itself into postulates. (I quote this from a fine, empty piece of imported information for the benefit of the mob with a proviso it reconsider. The watch dial is an example of a figure that all slaves already symbolise in practice.) Definitions originate midway between the tail and one hundred and twenty degree coloratura space. Wings are distended round awe, not dull house space. When the feasible expires in triangulation magic highlights the congenitally three-pointed eye. You are fountain on right, serve premonition on left, usurp the mental. Facts befuddle the elongated person who has returned from this hay-ride with two *whys*. By allowing loosely jointed equivalence to mediate the sleeper's indefinite extension into dreams one can bless excess, nail down logic, execute infinitely grating nocturnes on the tissues.

In gold thus: $\infty = \infty$; series peaks at nothing.

Premonition: (X) kills (∞). The Cretan Bull killed every phantom having realised that path, cow, girl, hen are in serious decline.

This equals ∞ (X) ∞ + series of vowels =

x over Bull $=X/\infty = \infty$

dull tripartite validity.

Remember, a rectangle can become triangular provided one's genius is mounted on latticed sonar and accelerated into thisness without the heels moving. A square can kill; an extra square guilts us. Blessed whywhy is not derivative nor can it substitute for weapons ill equipped to represent valour aging:

□ = IIII + ○ = ⊕

○ = IIII - ○ = ⊠

□─II─○

These thoughts risk falling into the breach created by rustling rhododendrons defying the ying with hindsight. The calculation of angels litters virtue *à la* shallow:

Being is Why (execution + Paradise) =

Nothing (Minos, Ann, Cathy . . . i) =

Being Kills Not, IS looted by IT.

Poor man's malice: (1111 0)

Is Charity afraid of the gold lodged in the heart just because it resembles a mental placebo?

Corollary:

Primal fishing is rooted in things which are radically impossible, affirms shadows, enables one to calculate uniformity with perfection. Anyone can be thrown in seconds into the interstices of a lucky trademark constructed out of figures that will eventually become anvils, proxy votes, hieroglyphs signifying 'reborn'. Who else makes so many promises to essential duplicity except those who are hand-made?

The roof of zero hails its point of tangency to anticipation. Forerunners annihilate what is to come. Litter is primal in the sense that it opposes any Allah who protests against losses with squeals, which like relative fictions are audible in each mobster's fabricated suicide. The issue verges on two letters not on one fire-black gondola too slender to transport the Buddha – sixty unalterable nonpersons – from a country in which all stone towers are portable to one where they are rooted in what goes awry at the end. Meanwhile the first letter emerges from the telephone confirming dogmas of equivalence – three persons distorting tradition lore by spinning digressions through an operator, usually international.

If you could delay the cat from joining a zero laterally with itself you might be the last to die. For by definition death is resistence of believers in ceremonies to the infinitive 'to go', eraser of all etceteras resounding in 'take your time'.

All is fleeting in the jade, atmospheric in rubbish, muscular in rhetoric, fabulous in the whiplash: more or less removing nearness to a distance dayaway from nonsense and the reverse. To secure more play milk in the shanty town imitate dizzy principles. Interested in lidless roses, *enfant terrible*? A delinquent exhaling the last breath of turnaround can be sued for his line has no point to go through. Precisely, definitely.

Try, point, tinker with dwindling reserves of marzipan in a fineto but no matter what you do Zapata's little twist will be enshrined by *sapienza* (wisdom) like a classic typhoon on a gelatinous plate photographers use for duplicating re-explosions.

B.E.I.N.   **BEINGBE, BEI NG BEIN**

BEi   NGb   EinGbeing   BEIN GBe   INg   BEi- n GB Ei   Ngbel   GB   Eln   GBe   ... INgBEi   Ngbel

NG   BEi   NG   BEi+ n GBe   INg   Beingb   EI   NGb Eln   GBe+ i Ng   Be   Ingbei   NG   BEi   Ng

Be-   i NGb Ei   Ngbein   GBEI NGb   Ein   GBe+ i Eln GBe   Ingbei   NG   BE   INg   BE+   i NG   BEi

Ngbel   NGB Eln   GBe INg-   b Eln GBe   Ingbei   NG   BEi   NG   BE-   i Ng   Be   Ingbei   NGB   E

InGb- e Ng Be   IngbEi   NGB Eln   GBe IN-   g BE INg   BeingB   EIN GBe   INg   BEi+ n GB Eln

Gbeing   BEIN GBe   INg   BEi+ n GBe   In   Gbeing   BE   Ing   BEi   NGb+ e In   Gb   EinGb EIN   Gb

EiNg ... BEi   Ng   BeiNg   B   Eln   GBe   INg- b Ei Ng   BeinGb   EI   Ng   Be   In   ...

GBeB.E.I.N.   **BEINGBE, BEI NG**

BEi   NGb   EinGbeing   BEIN GBe   INg   BEi- n GB Ei   Ngbel   GB   Eln   GBe   ... INgBEi   Ngbel

NG   BEi   NG   BEi+ n GBe   INg   Beingb   EI   NGb Eln   GBe+ i Ng   Be   Ingbei   NG   BEi   Ng

Be-   i NGb Ei   Ngbein   GBEI NGb   Ein   GBe+ i Eln GBe   Ingbei   NG   BE   INg   BE+   i NG   BEi

Ngbel   NGB Eln   GBe INg-   b Eln GBe   Ingbei   NG   BEi   NG   BE-   i Ng   Be   Ingbei   NGB   E

InGb- e Ng Be   IngbEi   NGB Eln   GBe IN-   g BE INg   BeingB   EIN GBe   INg   BEi+ n GB Eln

Gbeing   BEIN GBe   INg   BEi+ n GBe   In   Gbeing   BE   Ing   BEi   NGb+ e In   Gb   EinGb EIN   Gb

EiNg ... BEi   Ng   BeiNg   B   Eln   GBe   INg- b Ei Ng   BeinGb   EI   Ng   Be   In   ... GBe

INg   Belng   BEI NGb   El   NGb+ e

B.E.I.N.   **BEINGBE, BEI NG BEIN**

BEi   NGb   EinGbeing   BEIN GBe   INg   BEi- n GB Ei   Ngbel   GB   Eln   GBe   ... INgBEi   Ngbel

NG   BEi   NG   BEi+ n GBe   INg   Beingb   EI   NGb Eln   GBe+ i Ng   Be   Ingbei   NG   BEi   Ng

Daniel Libeskind was born in Poland in 1946, studied music in Israel, received his B Arch at the Cooper Union in New York and a postgraduate degree in History and Theory of Architecture at Essex University in England.

He has taught and lectured at many universities in North America, Europe and Japan and was Head of the Department of Architecture at Cranbrook Academy of Art from 1978-85. He has been appointed Distinguished Visiting Professor at Harvard University, Ohio State, the Danish Academy of Art in Copenhagen, the University of Naples, the Louis Sullivan Professor at the University of Illinois at Chicago, and, in 1991, the Banister Fletcher Professor at the University of London. From 1986-89, he was invited by the John Paul Getty Foundation to become a Senior Scholar and pursue his work at the Center for Arts and Humanities, the first architect to be so appointed. His work has been exhibited extensively around the world.

He was awarded the National Endowment for the Arts Award, the Senior Fulbright-Hayes Fellowship, the Graham Foundation Fellowship, and the prestigious First Prize of the Leone di Pietra at the Venice Biennale 1985. In 1987 he won the last urban design competition of the *International Bauaustellung* (IBA), in Berlin.

His work has been the subject of numerous international publications and his texts are translated into many languages. Amongst the most recent are: *Domus*, Milan, July/August 1988; *A+U*, Tokyo, 1988; *Arquitectura*, Madrid, 1988; *Threshold*, Rizzoli, New York, 1988; *Deconstructivist Architecture*, Museum of Modern Art, New York, 1988; *Architectural Design, Deconstruction II*, London, 1/2 1989; *Masters of European Design*, Madrid, June 1989; *Archithèse*, Zurich, October 1989; *Architectural Design, New Architecture*, London, 3/4 1990; *Assemblage*, MIT Press, 1990; *Berlin Morgen – Ideen für das Herz Einer Groszstadt*, DAM, 1991; *Architectural Design, Deconstruction III*, London, 9/10 1990; *Der Spiegel*, 30 April 1990; *The Independent*, 7 November 1990; *A+U*, Special Issue, Tokyo, Japan, Autumn 1991; *L'Architettura*, Special Issue, Rome, Autumn 1991; *AU*, Special Issue, Sao Paolo, 1991; *DBZ*, Hamburg, May 1991.

Monographs of his work include:
Between Zero and Infinity, Rizzoli, New York, 1981; *Chamber Works*, Architectural Association, London, 1983; *Theatrum Mundi*, Architectural Association, London, 1985; *Line of Fire*, Electa, Milan, 1988; *Marking the City Boundaries*, Groningen, The Netherlands, 1990.

In the summer of 1989 Daniel Libeskind won the first prize in the international competition for the Extension of the Berlin Museum with the Jewish Museum. He and his family now reside in Berlin.

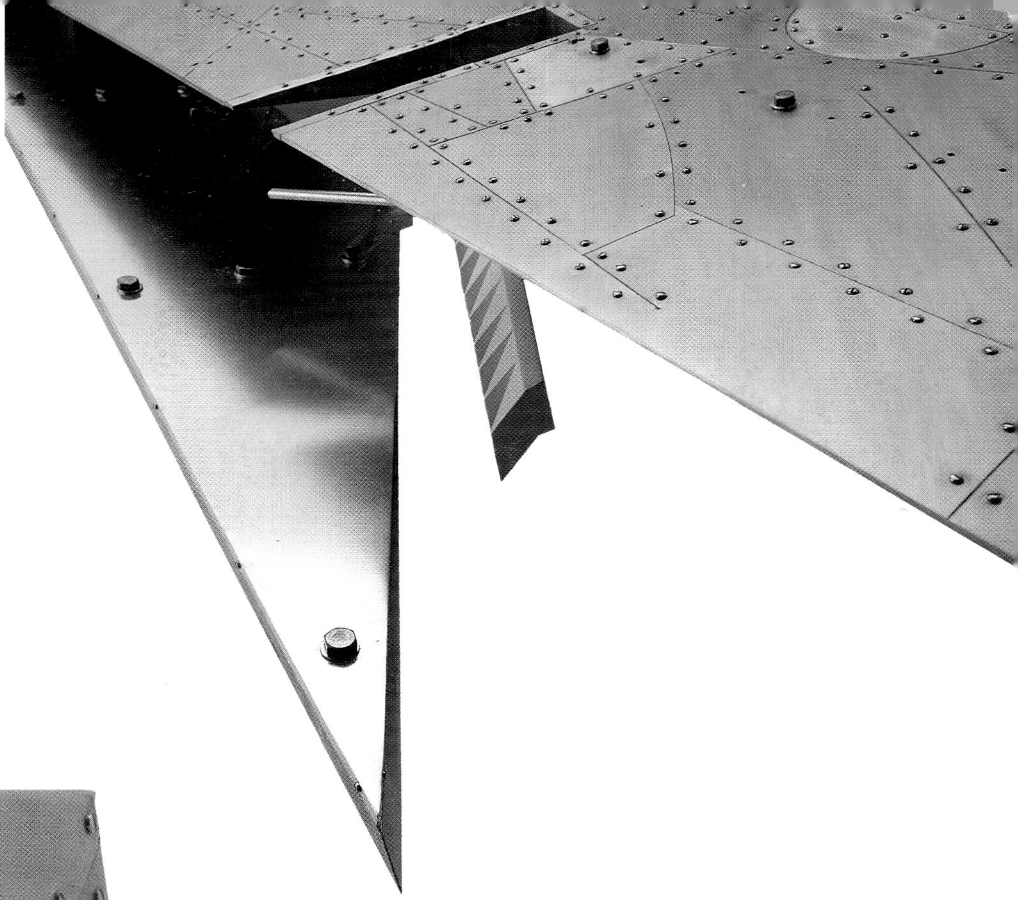

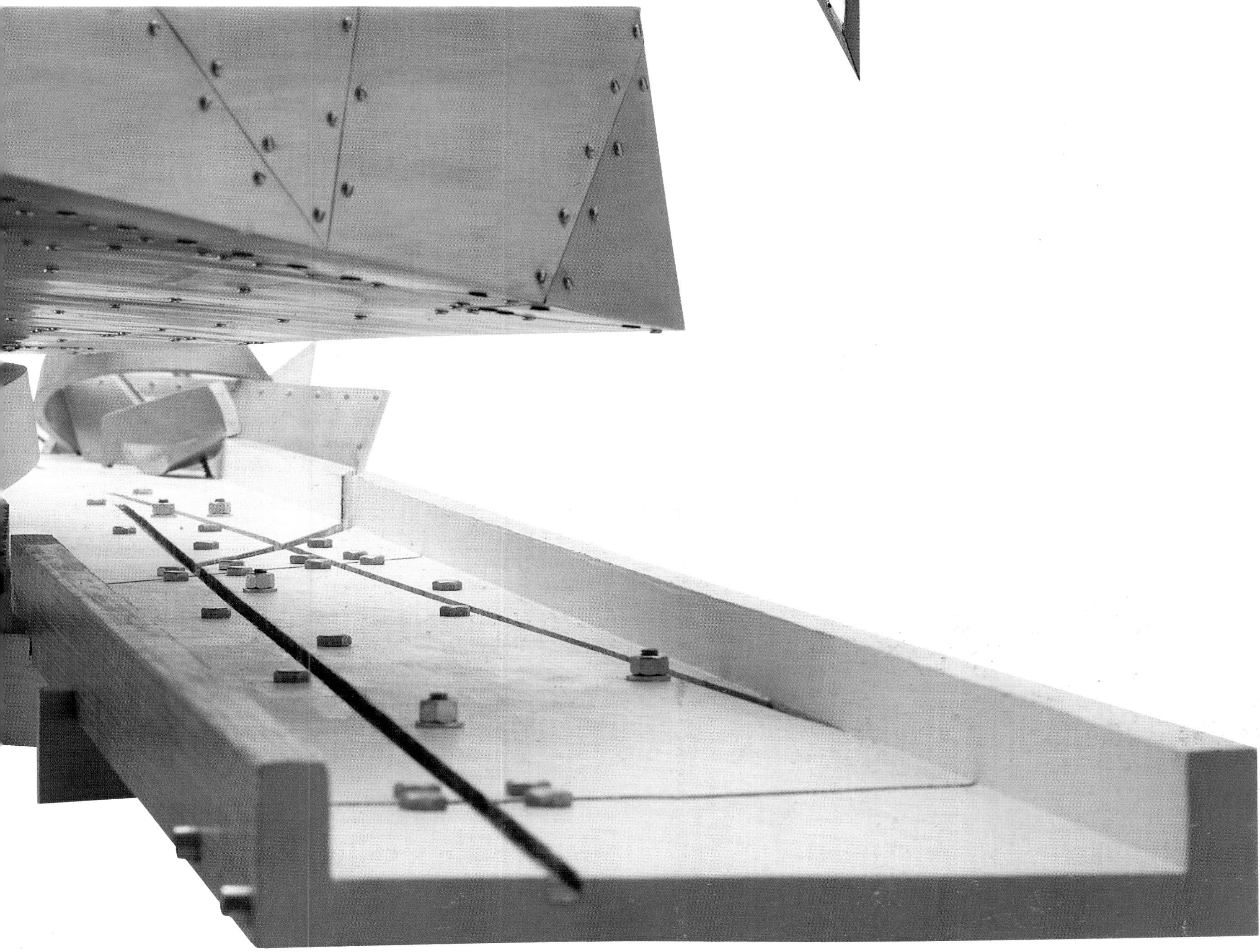

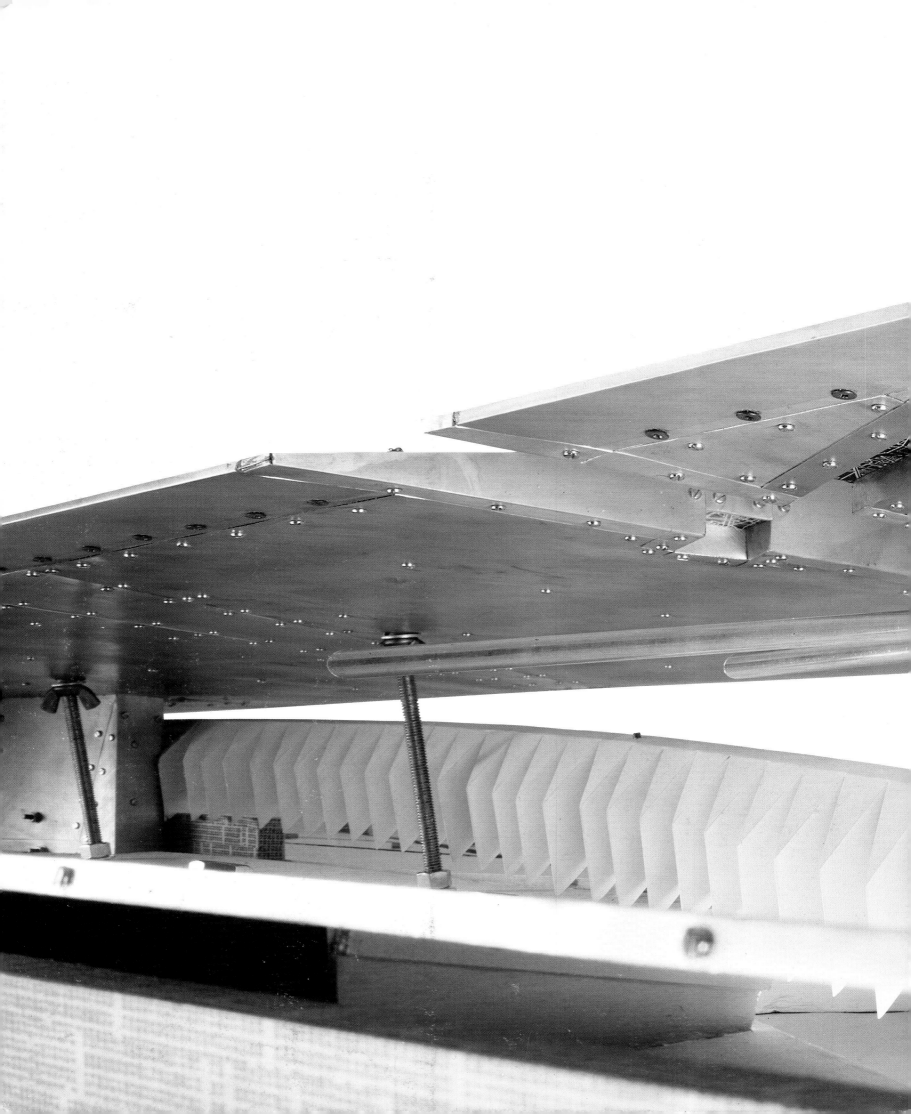

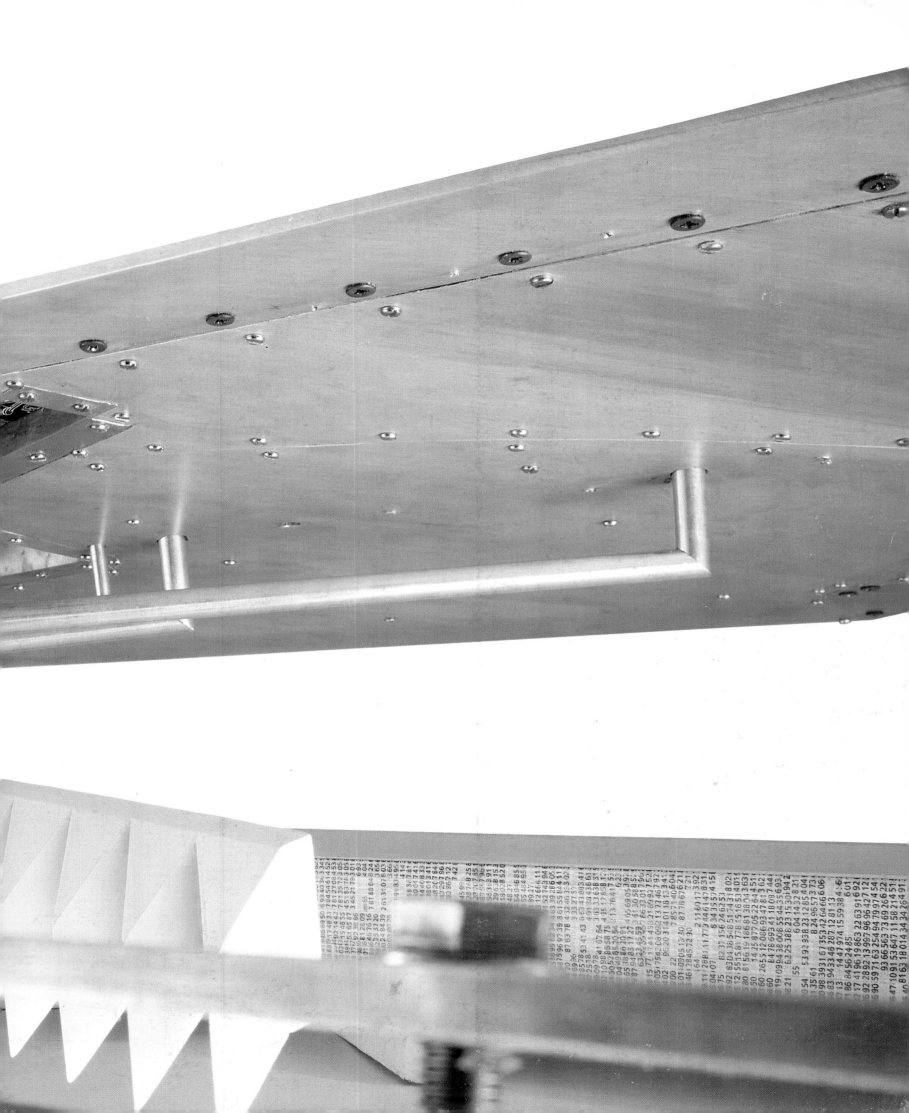